EVERYONE IS A READER

by Beverley Mathias

REACH

National Resource Centre for Children with Reading Difficulties

Published by REACH: National Resource Centre
for Children with Reading Difficulties

Originally published 1998

Produced by Signpost Books

Printed and Bound in Great Britain by
Biddles Ltd, Guildford and King's Lynn

ISBN 0 948664 20 7

REACH gratefully acknowledges the financial support of
the Paul Hamlyn Foundation

PREFACE

Petunia the Goose found a book. She knew it was useful as she had seen a child taking one to school. Petunia felt proud and knowledgeable and carried the book around with her, but when the other animals asked her for answers to questions she couldn't help them because Petunia couldn't read. The knowledge she needed was in the book, but without the means to access it, Petunia was helpless. So she learnt to read.

This handbook is for all the Petunias everywhere who want to read, but find access to books difficult and daunting.

Petunia *was written and illustrated by Roger Duvoisin, and published by The Bodley Head.*

"He who owns Books and loves them is wise," repeated Petunia to herself. And she thought as hard and as long as she could. "Well, then," she said at last, "if I take this Book with me, and love it, I will be wise, too. And no one will call me a silly goose ever again."

So Petunia picked up the Book and off she went with it.

CONTENTS

INTRODUCTION

This handbook, one of a series published by **REACH**, is a guide for parents and teachers working with children who have special needs relating to reading, writing and communication skills. It will also be of use to carers in residential units, social workers and therapists.

Children who have difficulty reading still want to read and enjoy stories. There is no reason for them to be unable to find what they want; bookshops, libraries and schools have most if not all of the materials these children need. Sometimes it may take a little more time than usual to find the right material, and a little imagination may be necessary to match a child with a book they are going to enjoy.

The purpose of this handbook is to draw attention not only to the needs of children for whom reading is a struggle, but also to highlight some of the ways in which they can read, so that they do not always have to rely on print. Reading print with your eyes, listening to stories on sound tape with your ears, reading video stories using your eyes, using sign language to read aloud, and your fingers to read Braille, are all legitimate ways of enjoying literature.

The term 'special needs' covers a wide variety of conditions, problems and difficulties. For some children the only special need they have is for a little extra attention, others require anything from part-time to full-time assistance in class. The difficulty a child experiences developing reading skills may or may not be connected to some other condition, which in turn might have a bearing on what the child is offered to read in terms of format.

When teachers, parents and others involved with a child are struggling to find a reason for the child's learning difficulty it is tempting to give the problem a name. This is not always a good idea for the child as labels can cause as much harm as good. The word 'dyslexia' is applied to many more children than have actually been diagnosed as having the condition. Specific learning difficulty is a better way of noting that the child is having problems with learning to read, write and communicate.

Once it has been decided that a child does have a learning problem, then it is possible that the process of formally presenting a Statement of Special Needs (usually referred to as a 'statement') might be put into action. Although the details may vary between local authorities the process is roughly the same. The teacher, head teacher, staff member in charge of special needs (SENCO) and the parents discuss the child's needs and decide on a course of action. To begin with this will probably be an Individual Educational Programme (IEP), which will be assessed at regular intervals throughout the school year. Depending on the severity of the problem, it might be assessed weekly, monthly, every half term, at the end of every term, or once a year. This is the beginning of the statement. There are usually five to seven stages to go through before the final statement is presented to the authority. Some children never progress beyond this first IEP because the learning problem is dealt with in the classroom with help from the SENCO and, perhaps, a classroom assistant. Other children might need outside intervention for a short period - perhaps speech therapy, visits from an Educational Psychologist, or a peripatetic teacher for sensory, intellectual or motor problems. The amount of intervention needed is reflected in the number of steps taken by the school before the authority is presented with a full statement. It is best to discuss the stages of statementing with the school to ascertain their particular procedure. However, regardless of procedure, the end result of a statement is that the child should receive the help requested for twelve months until the next statementing assessment.

There are some general areas of help which affect all children with learning problems, no matter what the cause. Differentiated text can help all children. This is an edition of a book which uses the same page layout and pictures but has a simplified and reduced text. The information is presented in a simple language, usually a large type face, and in an easily understood manner. The child can refer to the text for topic work, gain the same information as the rest of the class, but not be expected to struggle through the full text. The ability to listen is a skill which sometimes evades children with special educational needs. Using storytelling can help with listening skills, oral skills in relating events, and aural skills in comprehending what has been said. Regular sessions of oral storytelling as well as sessions of reading aloud help to develop listening ability, which in turn helps the expansion of language. For children who have difficulty with letters and lines which appear to 'jump' on the page, a selection of colour overlays can help. Ordinary plastic filing sleeves can be cut into squares and placed over print so that the child can experiment with the colour combination which works best.

This handbook includes a brief summary of the major problems that can affect reading ability - visual loss, hearing loss, learning problems, emotional and behavioural difficulties, delay in language development, physical and motor difficulties, intellectual problems - but makes no attempt to focus on any one condition. There are so many variables within conditions, syndromes, illnesses etc., that it is possible only to generalise using the major headings of visual, hearing, learning, emotional or behavioural, motor and language difficulties. At the end of each section is a brief list of books which have proved useful when working with that particular group of children. The full bibliographic details are contained in the index.

There are also two general sections; one on language development in children and the other on ways in which teachers and parents can offer supplementary help to children struggling to learn to read.

The fully annotated alphabetical index of titles includes all those mentioned in the text. There is also a listing of organisations.

CONDITIONS THAT MIGHT AFFECT READING ABILITY

A lack of reading ability is not necessarily a corollary of a specific condition. Many children with quite severe motor difficulties have no problems with reading. Children with sight or hearing difficulties are increasingly showing that with the right assistance they too can and do read at around the same time as other children. However, to be able to help children with specific difficulties, is it necessary to have some knowledge of how certain conditions can affect a child's ability to learn to read, write and use language for communications. The following is a summary of some of the major problems faced by children, which will hopefully provide help in understanding a child's fears, frustrations and anxieties. Throughout this section the personal pronouns 'he' and 'she' are used interchangeably.

VISUAL LOSS

Very few children are totally blind; most have some degree of sight, not enough, perhaps, to read print, but sufficient to distinguish light from dark. Because of the wide range of conditions that can affect sight, it is important to talk to the child to find out what he can see, whether he uses print only, print and Braille, or only Braille. In some conditions the size of type face is important; with others it is the contrast between paper and print. There are some general criteria which can be applied when looking for printed material for children with poor sight.

Large print is important to children with sight problems, but the spacing between lines and letters (the leading) is of equal importance. Most large print editions use a type size of between 16 and 20 point with leading of between 18 and 22 point.

Using this a guide it is possible to find some titles published by trade publishers which have the same size and clarity of print. Although there are no picture books specifically published as large print, there are numerous titles where the type size, page layout and leading make the book suitable for use by a child who has a sight difficulty.

Some children may be able to read good, clear, large print, but are unable to distinguish colour very easily. It is important that the colour contrast between paper and print is such that the image remains clear. This doesn't necessarily mean black print on white paper, as white can be too stark for someone with poor sight. Dark grey print on cream paper, and black print on yellow paper are much easier to read than a dense black print on shiny bright white paper. Illustrations need to be clear, but not necessarily large. Primary colours and clear black lines are often the best, as attractive muted shades can be very difficult to see clearly.

Jamie the great? He yelled a lot, but he was tough.

If we were wrestling, he would scream sometimes so I thought I had really hurt him, but he would never give up, never. And he would do such crazy comic falls that you'd wonder how he kept from breaking his neck. Jamie was a show-off and a clown, there was no doubt about that. And most of the time it was funny.

I stretched out on the play room floor and
for Martha. She coul

once again Sophie noticed how he seemed to melt into the shadows wherever he went. His feet made no sound at all, even when he was walking on gravel.

Suddenly, they were right up close against the back wall of the great Palace. The BFG's head was level with the upper windows one flight up, and Sophie, sitting in his ear, had the same view. In all the windows on that floor the curtains seemed to be drawn. There were no lights showing anywhere. In the distance they could hear the muted sound of traffic going round Hyde Park Corner.

The BFG stopped and put his other ear, the one Sophie wasn't sitting in, close to the first window.

"No," he whispered.

"What are you listening for?" Sophie whispered back.

"For breathing," the BFG whispered. "I is ⟩le to tell if it is a man human bean or a lady ⟩ the breathing-voice. We has a man in there. ⟩ortling a little bit, too."

⟩le glided on, flattening his tall, thin, black-⟩ked body against the side of the building. He ⟩e to the next window. He listened.

⟩No," he whispered.

⟩e moved on.

⟩his room is empty," he whispered.

⟩ listened in at several more windows, but at ⟩one he shook his head and moved on

If a child has access to an electronic reading machine, the size of print and the colour of the page won't matter. These machines are generally found in specialist schools for children with sight loss and in some public libraries, but are not conducive to quiet, private reading. The machine will read the text aloud in a mechanical voice, which means the reader must sit alongside the machine, although sometimes headphones can be used which allows a degree of privacy. The machine can't turn the pages, so at the end of each page there is a verbal instruction asking if the reader wishes to continue. The more expensive models of these machines can read text onto sound tape.

At school the child might be given a closed circuit television (CCTV). This is a form of video camera mounted under a high resolution monitor. Beneath this is a sliding table which moves from side to side and forwards and backwards. A book, page or object is placed on the table and the image is projected onto the monitor screen. The size of the image can be adjusted to suit the user. For children this means that not only print but also items such as maths equipment, tadpoles in a jar, small toys, leaves or any other item being used as a teaching aid, can be placed on the table for the child to enlarge and view on the screen. Although very effective, it can be tiring to use.

A child with tunnel vision, no three dimensional sight, no peripheral vision, or a degenerative condition, needs to be offered a wide range of printed materials to discover which is the easiest for them to handle. Often the use of an aspheric magnifier (glass dome in a plastic ring) can open up a whole new world of print to a child eager to read alone. Although it fragments the text as it is moved across the page, many children prefer this to a bar magnifier, or an adjustable round magnifier. The aspheric magnifier can be put in a pocket, allows for private reading, and is less obtrusive than other forms of magnification.

Whether a print or Braille user, children with sight difficulties are just as eager as sighted children to read a range of materials including popular titles, classics and pulp fiction. **Sometimes the major difficulty faced by the child is not the reading itself, but access to something to read.**

There is now an ever increasing range of titles available for children in commercially produced large print. Most of the range is suitable for children who are fluent readers aged between eight and twelve years. There is very little available for children who are just starting to read (early fluent readers). Large print for children is produced by **Chivers Press**. Chivers and Ulverscroft both produced fiction and non-fiction for adults, some of which might interest an older child or teenager. Most public and school libraries will also have titles published by Cornerstone and Windrush, two imprints no longer available. **The Royal National Institute for the Blind (RNIB)** may be able to help locate individual titles which have been enlarged by photocopier for use by specific students. Sometimes these are available for loan between schools. Note that before photocopying any book for use by a pupil, written permission must

ahead of me and I couldn'
turn back. It stopped be
when I fell in.'
'When you fell in?'
The way Adam kept repea
thing I said, it sounded as th
practising to be a parrot.
'That's right.'
'How did you get out?'
'With great difficulty. I thou
going to be stuck there until m
'Have you been sleepwalking
'I don't think so, but I wouldr
unless I woke up or somebody s
'What about the werewolf?'
'What about it?'
'You said the werewolf
somewhere near in your dream.
there when you woke up?'
'Of course it was. It ripped
pieces.'
'I'm b

be sought from the copyright holder, usually the publisher. Dictionaries and atlases are especially difficult to find, although **Oxford University Press** publish a large print dictionary suitable for primary school children.

Braille is not usually available at school unless the child is attending a special school or unit for children with sight difficulties. Braille is cumbersome and some children use it only as a means of learning to read English, using sound tapes for their leisure reading. Some schools for children with sight difficulties do have master copies of books which have been Brailled and can sometimes supply a copy. The **RNIB** produces a catalogue of Brailled books which can be helpful in finding particular titles, especially for school use.

ClearVision is a charity which produces picture books, fiction for early independent reading, and simple non-fiction in print and Braille. The Braille is on clear plastic pages, which are interleaved into the paperback edition of the book. This offers the reader the opportunity of sharing a book with someone else, and is an ideal way for a sighted parent and blind child, or sighted child and blind parent, to read together. There is quite a range of titles available that are suitable for children from preschool to mid-primary. A second charity, **Feel Happy**, also produces Braille and print, and adds a thermoform hand-painted picture of the chief character so that the child can build an image of the story. The **Feel Happy** range is not yet extensive.

Suggested Reading:

ALL THE BETTER TO SEE YOU WITH	*Margaret Wild*
CHARLIE'S EYE	*Dorothy Horgan*
CLASSIC FAIRY TALES	*Collins sound tape*
KIPPER'S BIRTHDAY	*Mick Inkpen (Moon)*
MR GUMPY'S OUTING	*John Burningham (Feel Happy)*
ROGER WAS A RAZOR FISH	*Jill Bennett (ClearVision)*

HEARING LOSS

The range of hearing loss varies enormously, from a child with intermittent loss to the child who is profoundly deaf. The decibel level and sound frequency which the child hears are very important. Some children lose hearing in the upper and lower registers only and can, with help, hear within the range of speech sounds. Others lose the mid-levels but retain upper and lower frequencies, which makes it extremely difficult to hear and understand speech. Beyond all odds, some children who have never heard clear speech develop the ability to converse with clarity despite the degree of hearing loss. Children with severe to profound hearing loss across all levels may never develop intelligible speech. Any hearing loss will have an effect on a child's understanding of language, and therefore on their reading ability.

There are conflicting beliefs when it comes to the way in which children with hearing loss should be taught, and whether or not they should use a signed language for communication. Some children are fitted with a cochlea implant, an electronic device embedded in the skull and connected to the cochlea, that allows sound to be transmitted to the brain. The sound is not natural, but is said to become clear and distinguishable with practice. It does not restore hearing, but does allow some degree of sound to be understood. When the equipment is disconnected at the end of the day, the child is still deaf.

Children with a significant hearing loss will hopefully be fitted with either one or two hearing aids. These usually magnify all sound, not just the sounds the child has difficulty hearing. With advances in hearing aid technology it is now possible to have aids that filter sound, or confine magnification to the frequencies the child cannot hear unaided. Whichever hearing aid the child has, it may not always be enough to assist them in understanding spoken language. It is also important to remember that lip reading is not an exact art, and only 40 percent of what is spoken can be read accurately, the rest is guess-work using context.

Children with a hearing loss are educated at a variety of schools. Some attend mainstream schools and need little, if any, assistance in class. Others, with a more severe loss, may attend a partially hearing unit in a mainstream school, or attend a mainstream school with a classroom assistant assigned to them. Those with severe to profound hearing loss may attend a specialist day or residential school for children with hearing loss. More children with hearing loss are now being supported in mainstream schools than ever before.

Within the school, the child's education can take a number of different directions. Some children thrive in the atmosphere of a mainstream school and become speech users. If parents want their children to use speech, they might send their child to school at an aural unit where natural aural teaching through listening skills takes place and the child is encouraged to speak, or to an oral school where speech is the preferred method of communication. An increasing number of parents, both deaf and hearing, want their children educated through sign language, usually **British Sign Language (BSL)**. **Signed English (SE)** is sometimes used to help a child to understand the structure of written and spoken English. SE uses BSL signs in English word order, and adds finger-spelling for plurals and other changes in word structure. **Sign Supported English (SSE)** uses BSL signs in English word order, without adding the finger-spelt changes, and the SSE user might not sign all words. Teaching through the medium of signed language is sometimes referred to as Total Communication (speech, gesture, sign, written) using BSL, Sign Supported English or Signed English. Some parents want a bi-lingual education for their children using BSL and English. Whichever method is chosen, it is of paramount importance that the child is given a means of communicating as soon as possible after diagnosis.

If a child cannot hear and understand speech, they must be offered an alternative means of communication. The obvious method is sign language as it allows the child to develop communication skills at the same pace as a hearing child. Learning to sign does not stop a child from learning to speak.

One of the major problems a signing child experiences is that once attending school they must be taught to read and write using their second language - English. BSL is syntactically and grammatically a complete language - the fourth largest indigenous language group in the UK - but its construction makes it unsuitable for printing as text. There are a small number of books available which use English and Signed English (SE) which are very useful to the child learning to read and to parents learning to sign.

Many deaf children find it difficult to understand metaphor, therefore the language of the texts they read needs to be simple without being simplistic. Reading non-fiction is often a preferred option as it is usually clearly laid out on well-designed pages with short bursts of text accompanying descriptive illustrations. This is not to say that the same children won't or don't read picture books and fiction - they do, but the selection needs to be made with care. Books with a clear storyline, text which is not dependent upon sound for effect, imagery which is not sound based, situations which are not ambiguous, and few, if any metaphors, will all help the child with a hearing loss to enjoy the printed word.

Although sound tapes are not an option for most deaf children, video stories can be a valuable extension of reading print. The visual story helps the child to understand, and the language is not lost if the video is captioned.

Whatever the method of communication, children with a hearing loss must be able to find books they can read.

Suggested Reading:

DAD AND ME IN THE MORNING	*Patricia Lakin*
THE FLYING FINGERS CLUB	*Jean F Andrews*
LANGUAGE FOR BEN	*Lorraine Fletcher*
OPPOSITES	*Angela Bednarczyk (signed)*
SIGN ME A STORY	*Royal School for the Deaf, Derby, video*

LANGUAGE PROBLEMS

All children who have trouble with reading, writing and communication have a language problem. However, children who are late in developing language, deaf children who are not given a signing language, and children who have a physiological difficulty with speech are at a disadvantage when it comes to learning to read.

Language is learnt by imitation, by listening and observing, and by experimenting with sound. If these stages are late, or do not occur, then the child does not have that reservoir of knowledge to call on when it comes to learning to decipher print. These children often need to be taken through the stages of developing language via the use of rhyme, repetition, and basic sound identification. If the problem is physiological there may need to be medical intervention as well.

Sometimes knowing and understanding the problem will help a child to overcome it. Stuttering can be helped by the recitation of poetry and by singing. While it will probably not cure the stutter, it can give the child sufficient confidence to try to speak clearly. Knowing that certain sounds are difficult to say can help a child to develop a vocabulary that allows him to avoid those sounds. A deaf child developing speech through reading and only partially hearing other people will sometimes use a very 'literary' language which, while good in itself, sets her apart from other children because of the formal nature of speech. This child can be taught more colloquial language.

Oral storytelling can help a child to develop speech that is clear and sequential. Hearing stories read aloud will help the child to understand speech, and increase listening skills. Reading aloud with a child assists the child to make the connection between print and speech, so that she hears and sees the word written on the page. Self correcting is something children need to be encouraged to do, while correction by an adult should be done with tact and understanding. Conversation helps by encouraging the child to experiment with words and gives confidence in self expression. The use of wordless picture books will help to develop language, narration skills, language sequencing, and expand vocabulary.

It is important for all children with problems related to reading, that what they read is of interest to them. This can mean finding sophisticated stories which use a simplified language.

Suggested Reading:

BEAR	*Mick Inkpen*
CLOWN ZIBO'S LETTERS	*Sensor Verlag*
COMPLETE PUZZLE WORLD	*Susannah Leigh*
THE DECEMBER ROSE	*BBC video*
MAKING FRIENDS WITH FRANKENSTEIN	*Colin McNaughton*
MEG AND MOG	*Puffin sound tape*

LEARNING PROBLEMS

It is frustrating to be unable to find age and interest-appropriate materials for children with learning problems. It is also annoying to look for exciting, lively stories for older children who have a low reading ability, and only be able to find books that are boring. There is no reason why either of these groups of children should not have books that are as colourful, interesting, exciting and readable as those being read by the children they see around them. This is particularly noticeable when a whole class is reading, and those with poor skills are seen to be flicking through the pages of a book they would like to read, but that is far beyond their ability.

These are the children who find it difficult to finish work because they don't understand what they have been asked to do; the children who find it almost impossible to read sufficiently well to complete a maths problem; and the children for whom reading is an incomprehensible task. They are often children who are struggling socially, and who watch what others do before joining in any activity. Many of the these children are not so severely affected as to need statementing, but they do need help. Sometimes this help may be no more than an occasional session of one-to-one work on a specific problem. Often parents can supply this help if given the right guidance by the school.

Children with learning difficulties vary from those who cannot recognise letters on the page to those who struggle but slowly achieve reading a page alone. There is no instant remedy to either difficulty, but there are ways of making it easier for the child. Children who are frustrated by print will begin to sit back and automatically assume they can't read any print at all. While they need to learn to read in order to survive in the outside world, it is sometimes more productive to take the print away and substitute a different form of reading for a while. This may be sound tapes or video stories of books they want to read. Wordless picture books are very useful in this situation, as the effort of telling the story helps with sequencing skills, narration, prediction and visual awareness. Away from the pressure of struggling with print, the child begins to listen and watch, taking in the story content and the spoken language, enjoying a past-time which has previously been denied them.

Going back to basics can also help, but it must be done with care and sensitivity. These children, particularly those of upper primary and junior secondary age, are well aware of their difficulties and are not well disposed to having them exposed to the light. There is material around that can be used to build confidence and skill. Wellington House (published by Thomas Nelson) is a language programme designed for older beginner readers with print reading material, language exercises and games. Each story is about the same group of characters and is a complete adventure or incident. Because the events, the illustrations and the concept are of interest to upper junior and lower secondary school children, they are interested enough in the content to want to do the work. Each step is self-motivating and easily achievable.

Scribed writing will also help to build confidence by allowing the child to see that she has knowledge of value stored in her brain, and that she can tell a story. As with removing print from reading, removing the necessity to remember how to form letters, how to spell and how to construct a written sentence, assists the child and gives a sense of satisfaction and achievement. Most children remember what they have said to a scribe, and will willingly 'read' back what is on the page; some will even want corrections made. It is important when scribing to use every second line, so that the child can copy the scribed text in his own handwriting if he wishes. The use of differentiated text also helps, especially for topic work. There are now a number of publishers producing this material - among them are Wayland, Watts and Dorling Kindersley.

Children who have dyslexic tendencies, speech difficulties and comprehension problems can be helped in much the same way. They are aware of having a problem, but can see no way of controlling or curing it. These children need to see the connections between reading-writing-speaking so that they can learn to listen and watch. Using tape-book kits, story videos, aural storytelling, scribing, will help to make sense of the problem. The child listens and looks simultaneously, taking in through a multi-media, multi-tactile approach as much language as possible.

It is important that the child feels comfortable with the work being offered. This doesn't mean pandering to the child, but providing material that is achievable within the time allowed, and that can be completed without frustration.

Suggested Reading:

DONALD AND THE SINGING FISH	*Peter Lubach*
MAKATON NURSERY RHYMES	*WH Smith video*
TEACHER'S PET	*Philip Wooderson*
THE TURBULENT TERM OF TYKE TYLER	*Puffin Sound tape*
WAY HOME	*Libby Hathorn*

EMOTIONAL AND BEHAVIOURAL DIFFICULTIES

There are many reasons why a child has emotional and behavioural difficulties. Some children may misbehave as the result of an outside cause - abuse, food allergies, lack of parental control, trauma, some upset at home. The period of misbehaviour may be short-lived or on-going. Whatever the reason or cause, the child presents problems in the classroom and probably at home as well. What is tolerated in one school may be considered serious misbehaviour in another. This is not necessarily a reflection on the school but more a combination of lack of personal control, peer group pressure, and outside standards. Some children and families will be less tolerant of authority than others and this will be reflected in the attitude of the children.

When the behaviour affects school work it is important to try and find the cause and tackle that first. Sometimes this can be as basic as asking that the child have a proper sight test, and an audio test for hearing loss. Children often don't realise there is anything wrong with their sight or hearing until tested and questioned. If there is something wrong, it can probably be corrected by medication, prescription glasses or hearing aids. Sometimes this is sufficient to curb the behaviour problem, but at least these two causes will have been eliminated.

Trauma experienced by a child as the result of a house move, new sibling, change in parental control, a step family, abuse, hospitalisation, illness, change of school and many, many other reasons, can be harder to pinpoint. A quiet talk with the child allowing the opportunity for fears and worries to surface, plus a word with the parent can help the child to struggle through the problem. More serious problems will need to be dealt with by outside agencies. Abuse of any form should be reported to the correct authorities. Picking up the pieces in class is a task demanding patience and understanding.

Where these difficulties impinge upon the child's willingness and ability to read and write the problem becomes similar to the child with learning difficulties. Taking away the pressure of print, even if the child is a skilled and competent reader, can relieve the child of the need to concentrate. Pleasure in reading can then come from sound tapes and videos. It is important, as with all children, to monitor progress and to be aware that as the child works through the trauma or problem she should be drawn back into a normal expectation of work and achievement.

Naughty children do exist. They thrive on pitting their strength against any form of authority, and can sometimes bully other children as a show of power. They often will not complete work, and will choose to disturb other children rather than concentrate in class. It can be hard to distinguish between the child who has a real problem and the child who is making a concerted effort to be as difficult as possible. A set standard of behaviour helps, in some schools this is called 'assertive discipline'. With a known system which the children realise is constant, most will adhere to the behaviour code given. Where this form of discipline is used it is important that it is applied to all children all of the time. Some naughty children respond to this form of behaviour control with only the occasional outbreak, others will continue to pit themselves against it.

Suggested Reading:

ABLE AUTISTIC CHILDREN (ASPERGER'S)	*Julie Davis*
AMBER BROWN IS NOT A CRAYON	*Paula Danziger*
AN ANGEL JUST LIKE ME	*Mary Hoffman*
HELP! IT'S HARRIET	*Collins sound tape*
I'M GLAD I'M ME	*Sesame Street video*
THE SUMMER-HOUSE LOON	*Anne Fine*

PHYSICAL AND MOTOR DIFFICULTY

Not all children with physical problems have difficulty with reading. Being wheelchair bound does not stop a child reading books, although it might make print reading difficult if the child has poor fine-motor control.

Children who are semi or quadriplegic may require assistance to read anything that needs control to turn pages or switch equipment on or off. If a child does not have full use of his arms and hands, but is mobile in other respects, there may be some degree of frustration and difficulty in using anything needing physical control. If a child has an intellectual difficulty as well as physical problems, the degree of help needed and the type of material suitable for their needs will demand much more thought.

The use of large-format books can help a child who has gross motor control as these books can be read on a table, the floor or a wheelchair tray. Taped books and books on video allow a degree of private reading not possible if someone has always to be on call to turn the pages of a printed book.

One of the most common frustrations faced by children who have physical and motor difficulties is the amount of time they are forced to spend in therapy sessions and hospitals. Most hospitals have teachers, and many that deal with long-term illness will have a school. Children who are hospitalised for long periods will be able to continue at least basic school work under the direction of the hospital teachers. But even with this help, children undergoing constant therapies, hospitalisation and frequent absences from school will find their education fragmented, and this disruption can have a detrimental effect on their reading skills.

Any child likes to empathise with the hero or heroine of a story, and it can be difficult to find good positive images of children with motor problems as characters in books.

Suggested Reading:

THE BEAR	*Tellastory sound tape*
MIGHTIER THAN THE SWORD	*Clare Bevan*
A NICE WALK IN THE JUNGLE	*Nan Bodsworth*
RUBY	*Maggie Glen*
SADDLEBOTTOM	*Jackanory video*
SEAL SURFER	*Michael Foreman*

LANGUAGE DEVELOPMENT IN CHILDREN

All babies are born with the skill to develop language and, in fact, all over the world babies begin by making the same sounds that fond families immediately recognise as words whatever their mother tongue might be. Language is developed by imitating sound, by hearing and experimenting. Thus small children make 'language' in tone and inflection long before actual words and phrases. Nonsense speech is part of learning to communicate. It has now been recognised that babies also learn an iconic language, using hand signs, gestures, and facial expressions to indicate needs and to communicate. Deaf children of deaf or hearing families, and hearing children of deaf families will develop naturally a bi-lingual communication system using spoken language and signed language.

From the moment of birth parents and the extended family look for and encourage response in the form of sound. Adults and children talk to babies knowing that the response will be physical rather than verbal. By the time the infant starts to speak she has already heard an amazing number of words. The child learning language through sign has also accumulated words through sight.

Words are a stimulus, and the nature of language, the way we use it, respond to it and acquire it, can affect our learning patterns later in life. Language, either spoken or signed, has an important part to play in the cognitive development of the child. The internalised speech of the child is used in play and in the form of long and sometimes quite involved monologues that are, in fact, spoken thought. The child who signs will stop play in order to sign the same type of monologue.

Language development is not a closed system but builds as an amalgam of context, social and sensory skills, and motor abilities. The infant builds up a relationship with her caretaker, be it parent, sibling, child minder or carer, and through this relationship gradually learns about language and how it is used in the community into which she has been born. As the adult interprets the child's sounds and signs, so the child gains a knowledge of object, sound and vision connections, and learns the intention of language as a naming system. As the child responds in increasingly recognisable speech or signs, so the child will try to explain unknown images and objects. The child will apply what is known to the unknown. A two year old whose knowledge of wheeled objects was limited to her buggy, the family car and the toy cars of her older brother used this stored information when she first saw a person wearing roller skates and commented 'Look, car boots'.

Ages and stages of development are not necessarily in the same time scale for all children, but they are a way of measuring development. Most children begin making babble conversation at around nine months of age, followed by recognisable sounds and single words at around twelve to fifteen months. By two years of age, children are beginning to socialise with language, uttering two or three word phrases. Whole sentences appear at between two and three years, together with the 'why' stage and the dreaded 'no'. At this point in language development, the child begins to use monologue to try to make sense of the world and of actions. By the age of three most children are fluent in speech and are developing a more complex sentence construction with an ever-increasing vocabulary. They begin to use abstract speech and can explain feelings, attempt an argument, and reason at a very simple level. At four many children are initiating conversation with others, and are able to take part in discussion.

All preschool children should develop through these stages, but for various reasons some do not. Children who have not acquired a reasonable vocabulary and who have not developed more than two or three word phrases are going to be at a disadvantage when they reach school. These are the children who are at risk of having difficulties in learning to read and write.

Children need to be spoken to, to be listened to, and to feel that adults want to hear what they have to say. A conversation with a young child should be enjoyable to both the adult and the child, and should incorporate a certain degree of correction, stimulation and expansion of language.

Josh (3)   *'I be go to park.'*

Mum   *'You'd like to go to the park would you?'*

Josh   *'Coat. Go now.'*

Mum   *'Not yet, I must finish the washing first.'*

Josh   *'Washing finish, coat on.'*

Mum   *'Yes, the washing's finished, get your coat on.'*

Later on there will be an expansion of language and an ability to use phrases, concepts and constructions heard in adult conversation.

James (7)   *'You can't do this, you're too small.'*

Isabel (4)   *'I want to try.'*

James   *'You'll never be able to do this.'*

Isabel   *'Mum, he's winding me up again.'*

If for some reason a child does not develop speech, she must be given another form of communication as quickly as possible. The obvious form is sign language. For children of deaf parents this is probably their first language and they will learn it bi-lingually together with English. For the deaf children of hearing parents it is a more difficult decision to use sign language as it becomes the child's first language and the parents' second. These children, too, must be bi-lingual.

Children who have severe learning difficulties and whose condition means it is very hard for them to develop speech can also be taught to use a signed language. One of these is Makaton, a system that allows the child the ability to converse at a simple level. However, if it becomes evident that the child will be a sign language user, it is important that a reassessment is done to see if the child would be better with a well developed and developing signed language such as British Sign Language (BSL). As many Makaton signs are based on BSL the switch is not traumatic, but allows the child a far greater vocabulary.

The use of a signed language does not deter a child from developing speech. If anything, it can enhance speech development as the child is already communicating and understands that language has a structure. The pressure of using speech as a sole means of communication is taken away, because the child knows he can make himself understood by using signs *or* speech.

Where a child has a severe loss of sight the need for language is different. Because she must understand the world around her, a blind child needs a well-developed descriptive language which, while not dependent upon visual clues, gives her the means of 'visualising' objects. There needs to be a multi-tactile approach to learning, using touch and smell to 'flesh out' a description. She must be given the linguistic means of writing creatively with words which use visual imagery she may not know in practice.

Any child who, by the age of seven, is not using descriptive and narrative language to explain incidents in every day life, write creatively, read with meaning, and converse with understanding, might need some teaching intervention.

HELPING A CHILD TO BECOME A READER

Developing the habits of a reader

Children learn many things by example. Seeing parents, older siblings, family members, friends, teachers and others in their immediate circle reading and enjoying books will influence the child to copy the activity. However, some children will need additional assistance to become fluent independent readers.

A child can be helped to develop the reading habit by being read to from an early age. Understanding the way print works - left to right, top to bottom, front to back - is a big step towards understanding the marks on the page. Even knowing that a book has an author, an illustrator and a publisher is helpful. These are terms that can be used when reading with a child long before the child reads alone. It should not be assumed that the child will automatically learn these features of a book, and having known them once, retain that knowledge. When a child begins to write, the reminder needs to be made about where print starts and finishes, and who is responsible for the writing and production of a book. From the beginning, every child should see herself as a writer as well as a reader.

Every opportunity should be taken to use the print visible in everyday life to reinforce reading. Shop signs, product names, directions, locations, are all part of learning to read. Children are capable of identifying food and household items by their packaging long before they can recognise the words.

Stimulating language development

All talk is fodder to language learning. Children absorb information in the same way a dry sponge absorbs water. Once taken on board the language is stored away for use at an appropriate time, or sometimes at the most inappropriate time. The 'why' and 'no' stages are wonderful opportunities for stimulating language use. As no single-word answer will satisfy a child's question, the expansion of reasoning allows for an increase in known vocabulary. A single negative answer by the child gives the opportunity to ask the child for a reason. Of course the child will often be defeated by this and simply answer 'because', a repetition of the answer most often heard.

Rhyme, verse, songs and short stories are all ways of increasing language knowledge. Some of these will become part of life, short phrases will resurface under different circumstances. 'Will you walk a little faster, please', is easier to comply with if you know the next phrase is, 'said the spider to the fly'.

With older children there are games to play that will expand the child's vocabulary. Playing 'I Spy' in the car will help with naming and initial letters, a board game based on letters will assist with spelling. Playing a word game involving letter connections such as a new word beginning with the last letter of the previous one will help children with language construction.

Many children of school age have a poor understanding of the specific naming words of everyday items such as fruit, vegetables and bread. This can be helped by using a feely bag (a towelling tea towel sewn into a sleeve with elastic at each end). The child places a hand in each end and feels the items placed inside, then tries to identify them. There is plenty of play food on the market to do this with. A progression of this game can be used to identify shapes, textures and size.

Encouraging reading and writing skills

By the time she reaches junior school, the child who is struggling to learn to read and write is full of frustration, anger, lack of co-operation, shame and a sense of low self esteem. Everything the child attempts must be achievable, which means working in very small stages. There are a number of ways in which parents, friends and classroom assistants can help the teacher by supporting the child and building confidence.

The method used by **REACH** to help Year Three children (and older) is a system based on work done in America by Donald Graves (*Writing: Teachers and Children at Work*). It emphasises the child's known language and uses it to encourage story narration which is scribed, and made into a book which can then be read by the child. Spelling can be 'invented', that is, the child is encouraged to write down the word using the sounds heard.

This method works through a number of stages, the time taken depends on the child, the amount of time available for one-to-one assistance, and the skill of the adult scribe. It is always done in conjunction with the classroom teacher.

Stage One:

The child is asked the following questions which must be answered in complete written sentences. Reassurance is given to the child that spelling does not have to be correct. The response to the request is often, 'I can't write'. If the child is reminded that this is not a test but a way of finding out about him, the fear of failure is partially removed, and he is usually willing to be cooperative. The questions are spoken and written by the scribe, who might also need to assist the child verbally in framing the answering sentence. All the questions can be answered by a rephrasing strategy.

Saturday

I got up at 7 and got washed and dressed.
after Breakfast I went out and rode my Bike.
Beefore Lunch I talked to my dad Bout a puppy.
be Cause I want a dog.
I watched cartoons on tv and played with sistr
we all went to somer field on our Bikes.
After we did the shoping we went home and
cooked lunch. I helped mum with the
vegetables. then I took washout of the washing
machine. I went into my bed room and wrot
a Letter to my aunt. I drew a picture.
Just before I went to bed I had a barth.

1 WHAT IS YOUR NAME? *(many children can only spell their first name)*

2 HOW OLD ARE YOU? *(some children cannot write the number word)*

3 WHERE DO YOU GO TO SCHOOL?
(many children cannot write the school name)

4 WHAT IS YOUR FAVOURITE FOOD?
(this shows up common spelling errors)

5 WHAT IS YOUR FAVOURITE FOOTBALL TEAM?
(most can spell the football team)

6 WHAT DO YOU LIKE TO WATCH ON TV?
(shows up common spelling errors)

7 WHAT WOULD YOU LIKE TO BE WHEN YOU GROW UP?
(always very interesting)

Once the questions have been answered the child is asked to read them out loud. Nearly every child can accomplish this unaided, as they will remember what they have written. As each answer is read, the scribe writes it down *on a different sheet of paper*, not on the child's work. At the end of the session the scribe has a sheet containing the questions asked, and the child's answers. The child has a sheet with their own answers only. A short discussion on the content of the answers reinforces the child's understanding that the information given is valuable and interesting, but no comment is made on the spelling. Both sheets are put aside to be brought out at a later point to show the child how much progress has been made.

Stage Two

By using the language the child already has it is possible to interest the child in narrating a story. This might be imaginary, based around an event such as a football match, or even a toy which is shown to the child. The scribe writes exactly what the child says, without syntax or grammatical corrections. The child is then assisted with the task of reading it back, at which time the scribe and child will discuss the construction of the story to see if they can improve it. Most children will notice mistakes that make the story difficult to understand and many will not need prompting to make the necessary corrections. All the alterations and corrections are made by the scribe on the instruction of the child.

The story is typed up in large print as either short blocks of text or as separate lines. The printed text is cut and pasted onto one side only of A4 sheets of sugar paper (or similar coloured paper), and the pages fixed together. A blank piece of white paper is pasted above the text so that the child can illustrate the story. There must always be a title page showing the title and author. Hole punched and held with either string or tape, the books are quite durable. These books are usually only six or eight pages to begin with, but will expand with experience. The book can then be read to the class by the author (who will remember the text) and added to the class library.

Alongside the writing task the child is introduced to very simple stories, beginning with wordless picture books. These encourage the use of spoken language and allow the child to concentrate on telling a story from illustrations, at the same time learning or relearning how a book operates (left to right, top to bottom). With some children it can help them understand the need for care in sequencing a story if they can tell their version onto a tape. When they listen and look at the pictures again, they can often see what they have missed or perhaps interpreted incorrectly.

Parents can help by giving the child a plain scrap book and encouraging them to record special events, outings, and visitors in the book then illustrating it on the same page. Scribing can be done by an older sibling, parent, grandparent, or a friend.

A further part of this stage is to stimulate interest in reading by substituting print books in the child's book bag for taped stories with or without the printed edition. Instead of being asked to read aloud with the teacher, assistant, or parent, she can be asked to draw the beginning, end, and one event from the story she has read on tape.

Stage Three

Once the child is at ease with this form of reading and writing, the next stage is to encourage the child to write without the aid of a scribe. To begin with she narrates a story that is written down verbatim by the scribe, but in pencil on every second line. This story is discussed, reread and corrections made at the child's instigation. The scribe/teacher might also question sentence structure and discuss ways of improving the flow of the story. Once all this is achieved and the child is happy with the result, she is then asked to copy the writing in the spaces left and to read it back. This method helps in improving language structure and spelling.

Copying a dictated piece of writing also allows for the gradual improvement of handwriting skills. Because the story is familiar, most children can read back what they have dictated with very little help.

At this stage the print books offered for reading will progress from wordless books to stories with good illustrations and one or two lines of text on the page. Rhyming text, familiar situations, cumulative and repetitive texts are the best to use at this point. It is also useful to remember that a child will read about younger children if the book is presented in the right way. The most successful books are often humourous. Collections of simple poetry, particularly silly poems, are also invaluable.

At some point during the process of scribing dictated work onto every second line, the child will ask the scribe to 'rub out what you wrote'. This is a landmark day, as it shows that she has realised the writing is hers, and that she has the confidence to try it alone without the crutch of dictating to a scribe. She will then read what has been written on the page with more confidence.

The print offered in books can now become a little more complex, but must always be within the reach of the child without too much assistance. Preselecting books that will interest the child, and are within her skill level, helps to focus the child's choice. Sometimes very short stories in a collection will be useful, at other times she might be more interested in a humourous picture book. The tape books can now be removed from the book bag and replaced with print.

From this point on the child does the writing. It will be slow and laborious, and it is important to keep bolstering her self confidence. She will still want to make books, and these can still be typed once she is satisfied with the story. Editing is part of learning to write and should be incorporated from the very beginning, first in discussion and, at this stage, in correction. Any spelling mistakes should be discussed positively along the lines of how many letters and sequences are right rather than how many are wrong. The corrections should not be made on the child's text; this is too demoralising as at this stage probably every third word is incorrectly spelt. Place the corrections in order down the margin of the page, having asked the child's permission to do so. In discussion, she might want to change some of the story, or expand on some point. This should be done before any rewriting. The first draft is then re-written, re-read and re-edited before being copied out in good, clear handwriting.

Once there is some degree of confidence, a further step in organising and planning any writing - creative, report, letters - can be introduced. This is called brain-storming. The topic to be written about is placed in a circle in the centre of an empty page. Using lines from the centre,

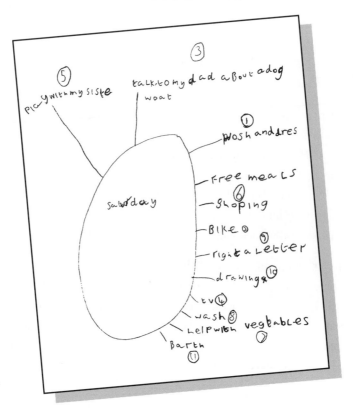

every idea, thought, or relevant word is put at the end of one of these lines. When the child is satisfied that all the ideas are written (or drawn), the various strands can be pulled together into separate blocks of words. Finally, the blocks can be used to write the piece.

The books offered to her for reading can now incorporate a greater degree of self selection. By presenting a range of titles, all within the reading ability of the child, she learns to select for herself the style of writing she prefers and the type of story that interests her. The five finger test can also be introduced at this point. This commonly used test can work in two different ways. In the first application the child begins to read and leaves a finger under the first word that they cannot understand or read. If they have four fingers and a thumb on words on the first page of text then the book is too difficult for them. A different way of applying the test is to spread the hand over the page and then read the words under the thumb and each finger. If three or more words are unknown, then the child should choose a different book.

Stage Four
As writing becomes more fluent, correction can be passed over to the child. She should be encouraged to continue to brainstorm, and when the writing is complete, to circle any words which she feels might be incorrectly spelt, and indicate any phrasing that she feels is wrong. Punctuation should also be included in this. Again, the response of the assistant should be positive, focusing on the letters and constructions that are right, and pointing out where changes might need to be made. With the child's permission, the scribe/teacher/assistant can write corrected words in the margin of the page. This draft, as with the earlier work, needs to be re-written, re-read and re-edited before being copied out as finished work.

Dictionary work will be taking place within the class, and this should be encouraged. Sometimes with a child who is a very poor speller, a 'poor speller's dictionary' can help, but it is not a good idea to use it while a child is struggling to read, and it cannot help a child who doesn't know initial sounds. Far better to encourage the use of a good simple illustrated dictionary.

The selection of print reading is now a matter for the child, and although mistakes will be made and she will take books she can't read, she will also develop more as a reader if she is challenged occasionally. Parents should be encouraged to read to and with children so that they continue to hear and see the written word.

Games to encourage language use

There are now many word-based games available commercially. Picture dominoes, picture matching, word pairs, are all useful as they encourage spoken (signed) language and the extension of knowledge of language concepts such as 'up', 'over', 'beside'. Games where words can be built onto boards using loose tiles or loose individual letters on the table top will help with learning initial sounds and vowel/consonant blends. The feely bag can be used to help a child learn specific nouns. Floor jigsaws which include words are handy, especially for older children. Word games such as word searches, elementary crosswords and spelling games, will assist in extending the child's vocabulary. Verbal word games such as thought association, memory based games and listing items that are similar, whispers, etc., are fun and can be played with small groups.

Book formats

Books are not necessarily print on paper. For children with reading difficulties books need to be in the format that is most appropriate to the child and easiest for the child to read. Children need to be able to read with their eyes, their ears, their hands and their fingers.

Print:

Print on paper is the most common format for a book. it can be hard bound or paperback, loose leaf, spiral bound, zig-zag or some other form beside the more usual square or oblong of bound pages. Print comes in various sizes and type faces. Some books have illustrations, some do not. Within the range are picture books without text, picture books for older readers, movable books (pop-up, flap, squeak), fiction for early independent readers, fiction for juniors and fiction for teenagers and young adults. Print books for readers often come in publisher-generated series using the same format, length of text, style of binding; or books which feature the same characters. Series can be written by one author or a number of different authors. Most series are identifiable by a distinctive logo.

One important product from print publishers is large print books. Originally the province of children with sight difficulties, these editions are also welcomed by children with reading problems because the size of type, and the space on the page are conducive to reading without too much of a struggle.

Large format picture books and non-fiction are very useful for children with sight problems and also for children who are finding reading difficult. The novelty of the size and shape make them interesting to handle, and the size of print takes away any struggle to recognise letter shapes. These books are also good for group work as they can be easily seen by a number of children seated on the floor.

Sound Tapes:
Books which have been recorded onto sound tape are invaluable to the struggling young reader with or without an accompanying print edition. They permit the child to enjoy reading without the pressure of deciphering print. These tapes are useful in a number of situations. They allow a motor-disabled child to read alone using a tape recorder, a blind child to read alone, a child to read in the car without suffering from motion sickness, or they can just be enjoyed as a means of listening to a story told by someone other than a parent, carer or friend. Used in conjunction with the print edition, these taped books can assist a child with reading by allowing him to listen and follow the text. However, care must be taken that the taped book and the printed book text match exactly.

Books on Video:
More and more children's stories are being filmed either as full scale movies, as animated stories, or as stories showing illustrations with a voice over. All of these are a useful and satisfying way of reading.

For the deaf child this form of book is vital. An increasing number of videos have been close captioned, allowing the deaf child to read while watching. To access some close captions a special decoder is needed, with others, captions are included on the open screen. Videos which have been signed are more difficult to find, most of them coming from schools and colleges teaching deaf children, but it is possible that within the near future a small range might be produced commercially.

Signed Texts:

At the moment there are eight picture books available from British commercial publishers which include signed captions or signed text. These use either Sign Supported English or Signed English, not British Sign Language. It is hoped that an additional range of signed picture books will be available from trade publishers in the near future.

Braille and Tactile Text:

Braille text for children is usually produced by schools that cater for Braille users, and is not often offered for sale to public libraries or individuals. Braille can be borrowed for home and school use by contacting the Royal National Institute for the Blind. The National Library for the Blind has Braille/text books. A new innovation is Moonshare (Moon/text), which is the use of a raised image which incorporates part of the written shape of a letter. This method of reading is sometimes used with people who lose their sight after learning to read print.

ClearVision is a method of interleaving Braille on clear plastic into unbound picture books, fiction and non-fiction, which is then spiral bound. There is now a wide range of titles available on subscription direct from ClearVision. Feel Happy is a second organisation using this form of publishing. They add one or two thermoformed illustrations of the main character to the Brailled edition of the book. These editions are lent or sold together with a print copy of the book and tape describing the illustrations.

Every child needs to be encouraged, stimulated and assisted to read independently. For most children that means reading print, but for those for whom print is an insurmountable problem there must be other ways

A	B	C	D	E	F	G	H	I	J

K	L	M	N	O	P	Q	R	S	T

U	V	W	X	Y	Z

1	2	3	4	5	6

Braille

7	8	9	10

A	B	C	D	E	F	G	H	I	J

K	L	M	N	O	P	Q	R	S

T	U	V	W	X	Y	Z

Moon

and other means of accessing books. Children need to be able to find books which have the right story, the right level of understanding and the right format for their own individual needs. This means offering the child the facility to read with eyes, ears, hands and fingers in whichever combination is suitable and appropriate at that particular time.

REACH has many samples of all the book formats mentioned above. They are available for browsing and assessment at any time during the Centre's opening hours

BIBLIOGRAPHY

This bibliography is a guide to the type of material available for children with reading and language difficulties. It is not intended to be a definitive list, but a listing of titles mentioned in the text, plus many more that are suitable to use with, and be read by, children with various difficulties relating to reading and language. A proportion of the titles listed feature children with a physical, sensory or intellectual difficulty, thus giving the reader a positive image of himself. Age interest and age reading levels are indicated, but these should be used as a guideline only, as many children will read both above and below their chronological age if the material offered is of interest.

Most of the titles listed are in print and should be available from good bookshops. Specialist children's bookshops can be found in many large cities and towns. All of the titles listed including those that are out of print, should be available for loan from local public libraries, and many of them will be in school library collections, or education authority professional development centres. Because this Handbook is meant to show the many ways in which children read, some titles are listed only as a sound tape or a video. Only one edition of each title is included, although other editions might be available.

The age interest and age reading levels are shown as follows:

Age Interest	Age Reading
PRESCHOOL	0-4 years
INFANT	4-7 years
LOWER PRIMARY	7-9 years
UPPER PRIMARY	9-11 years
LOWER SECONDARY	11-13 years
TEENAGE	13-16 years
ADULT	

The format of the book is indicated as follows:

Hardback **HB**	Braille **B**
Paperback **PB**	Sign language **SL**
Sound tape **S**	Moon **M**
Video **VHS**	Large Print **LP**

Where a story contains a character with a specific difficulty, or is in a format best suited to a particular need, this is indicated as follows:

Physical difficulty **P**	Visual loss **V**
Learning problem **I**	Hearing loss **H**
Language difficulty **L**	Emotional **E**

A typical entry is arranged as follows:

EVERYONE IS A READER **Beverley Mathias,** illus. Pauline Baynes
Reach 1998
0 948664 20 7
A quick reference source on the most common causes of reading disability, with helpful information, booklists and suggested teaching methods.
Adult. PB. P I L V H E

There is of course tremendous cross-over between the various areas of reading difficulty and the bibliography should be used to find titles that will appeal to the individual child. Thus large print, sound and vision should be used in conjunction with ordinary print, allowing the child to choose the medium most suited to her ability.

A

ABLE AUTISTIC CHILDREN - Julie Davies
CHILDREN WITH University of Nottingham Early Years Centre,
ASPERGER'S SYNDROME 272 Longdale Lane, Ravenshead, Notts NG15 9AH. No date.
No ISBN.
Written for the brothers and sisters of children who have Apserger's
Syndrome, and designed to allay fears and offer support.
Upper Primary/9-11years. PB. E.

ALL JOIN IN AND **Quentin Blake.** Read by Richard Briers.
OTHER NONSENSE Random Century Tellastory Audio.
A wonderful collection of rhymes and stories by Quentin Blake
gathered together into one volume. Includes Mr Magnolia.
Lower Primary. S.

ALL THE BETTER TO **Margaret Wild**, illus. Pat Reynolds
SEE YOU WITH Allen & Unwin (Little Ark) 1992.
ISBN: 1 86373 232 2.
Kate sees everything through a haze until the day she is
given glasses. Two identical spreads at the beginning and
end of the book show the difference in what Kate sees.
Infant/7-9 years. HB. V.

ALPHABET SONGS comp. **Marie Birkinshaw**, illus. David Pace
Ladybird (book and tape pack) 1996
ISBN: 0 7214 1861 9.
A printed collection of the words of well-known songs for
early childhood, plus a sound tape of the music.
Infant/7-9 years. HB. S.

AMBER BROWN IS **Paula Danzinger**
NOT A CRAYON Macmillan 1994
ISBN: 0 330 33143 4.
Justin moves to another area and Amber isn't sure she can
survive at school or at home without him.
Lower Primary/7-9 years. PB. E.

AN ANGEL JUST LIKE ME **Mary Hoffman**, illus. Cornelius van Wright & Ying-Hwa Ho
Frances Lincoln 1997
ISBN: 0 7112 1179 5.
Tyler wants an angel that looks like himself for the family
Christmas tree, not a pink one. He finds a black Father
Christmas and eventually is given a black angel.
Upper Primary/7-9 years. HB.

ANIMATED ALPHABET BBC video
A cleverly conceived moving film of the letters of the alphabet with the voices of children naming words and sounds. Over 400 words are used to animate verbs and adjectives.
Infant. VHS. L.

A-Z ANIMALS **Beverley Mathias and Ruth Thomson**, illus. Stephen Iliffe, Franklin Watts
1988.
ISBN: 0 86313 784 9
A photographic alphabet in sign language and text.
Lower Primary/7-9. HB. SL.H.

B

BABIES NEED BOOKS **Dorothy Butler**
Pelican 1982
ISBN: 0 14 022434 3.
Chapters about children and their reading from birth to six years. Although the bibliographic information may be out of date, the philosophy behind the writing is very current.
Adult. PB.

BEAR **Mick Inkpen**
Hodder 1997
ISBN: 0340 69829 2
A bear falls out of the sky into Sophie's cot and decides to stay. He causes havoc until a solution is found for his dilemma. This is a text and sound package.
Infant/7-9 years. HB. S. L.

BEAR, THE **Raymond Briggs**
Random House 1996
Tellastory tapes read by Ian Holm. Tilly makes the bear welcome in her home and reports progress to her parents who regard Bear as a figment of her imagination.
Lower Primary. S.

BFG, THE **Roald Dahl**
Thames Video Collection
Sophie saw the giant and has to be spirited away. She also discovers that not all giants are friendly, although they are all big.
Lower Primary. VHS.

BIG BAD PIG
Allan Ahlberg, Colin McNaughton
Walker (Reading Time) 1990
ISBN: 0 7445 1604 8
Absolutely ridiculous stories which play on rhyme and concept.
Lower Primary/6-7 years. PB.

BIG BROTHER DUSTIN
Alden R. Carter, illus. Dan Young
Albert Whitman 1997
ISBN: 0 8075 0715 6
Dustin has Down's Syndrome and is looking forward to the arrival of a baby sister.
Infant/7-9 years. HB. I.

BIG CLASS LITTLE CLASS
Francesca Simon, illus. Sonia Holleyman
Orion 1996
ISBN: 1 85881 189 9
Well-known fairytale characters mixed together into a story about school.
Lower Primary/7-9 years. HB.

BIKER
Anthony Masters, illus. Gary Rees
A & C Black (Graffix) 1997
ISBN: 0 7136 4561 X
A novel told in comic strip and prose about Terry who is desperate to show his father how good he is at motocross.
Lower Secondary/9-11 years. HB.

B IS FOR BEAR
Dick Bruna
Methuen 1977
ISBN: 0 416 93100 6
A classic ABC which uses bold colours, clear outlines and only lower case letters.
Preschool/0-4 years. HB. V.

BLABBERMOUTH
Morris Gleitzman
Pan Macmillan 1992
ISBN: 0 333 59501 7
Rowena Batts has a dad who sings country and western and is an embarrassment to her. She can't voice her complaints as Rowena can hear but not speak, and uses sign language to communicate.
Upper Primary/9-11 years SL.

BLITZ

Robert Westall, read by James Bolam and Susan Jameson.
Collins Audio.
Four stories set in World War II involving a plane crash, an air-raid shelter and other frightening but funny events.
Upper Primary. S.

BOYS ARE US

Shoo Rayner
Collins (Colour Jetds) 1998
ISBN: 0 00 675339 6
David's angelic looks win him the role of lead singer in a hot band.
Upper Primary/7-9 years. PB.

THE BOY WHO WOULDN'T SPEAK

Steve Berry, illus. Deirdre Betteridge
Annick Press, Canada 1992
ISBN: 1 55037 230 0
Owen doesn't speak, but he makes friends with the giants who live next door
Lower Primary/7-9 years. E.

C

CALLING TRACY

Clare Cherrington
Hamish Hamilton 1993
ISBN: 0 241 13276 2
Tracy's accident has left her with a limp. She finds it very difficult to return to school and to find a sport that will replace skating.
Lower Secondary/9-11 years. HB. P.

CAN'T YOU SLEEP LITTLE BEAR?

Martin Waddell, illus. Barbara Firth
Walker Books 1994
ISBN: 0 7445 3691 X
Little Bear tries every trick in the book to avoid going to sleep.
Lower Primary/7-9 years. Large format PB

CAPTAIN JONES AND THE GHOST SHIP

Ross Thomson
Orchard Books (Crunchies) 1997
ISBN: 1 86039 283 0
A crew of very unsuccessful pirates stumble onto an island laden with treasure.
Upper Primary/7-9 years. PB.

CHARLIE'S EYE　　　　**Dorothy Horgan**
Hamish Hamilton 1997
ISBN: 0 241 113681 4
Charlie is a lively girl who happens to have an artificial eye. She sees herself as 'normal' and doesn't understand what 'handicapped' means.
Upper Primary/7-9 years. HB. V.

CHILDREN AS WRITERS　　　**Chris Lutrario**
Harcourt Brace Jovanovich, USA 1992
ISBN: 0 7466 0058 5
A series of cards - subject, form, general - used as the basis for introducing children to writing in various genres.
Adult. PB.

CLASSIC FAIRY TALES　　　**Retold by James Riordan**
FROM THE BROTHERS　　　Read by Rula Lenska and Andrew Sachs
GRIMM　　　Collins Audio.
A wide range of traditional tales told in a way that encourages reading skills.
Lower Primary. S.

CLOCKWORK OR　　　**Philip Pullman**, illus. Peter Bailey
ALL WOUND UP　　　Chivers Press (Galaxy) 1998
ISBN: 0 7450 6010 1
A series of stories told by a novelist that mesh into a chilling tale seemingly dictated by the ticking of a clock.
Lower Secondary/9-11 years. LP.

CLOWN ZIBO'S LETTERS　　　**Sensor Verlag**
Munich 1994
ISBN: 1 85503 072 1
A tactile alphabet with upper and lower case letters, plus a coloured picture of an appropriate creature. This could be used by children with some residual sight.
Infant/0-4 years. HB. V.

COMPLETE PUZZLE WORLD　　**Susannah Leigh**
Usborne 1993
ISBN: 0 7460 1859 2
A collection of the first six titles in the Puzzle series. These demand a degree of visual skill.
Upper Primary/7-9 years. PB.

CRACKER JACKSON

Betsy Byars
Chivers Audio Books 1985
Cracker is alarmed when he receives an unsigned note indicating someone is in danger. Together with a friend he tries to rescue her.
Upper Primary. S.

CURSE OF THE EGYPTIAN MUMMY, THE

Pat Hutchins, illus. Laurence Hutchins
Chivers Press (Galaxy) 1996
ISBN: 0 7451 4958 8
The scout camp looks like being a disaster, but adventures abound.
Upper Primary/9-11 years. LP.

D

DAD AND ME IN THE MORNING

Patricia Lakin, illus. Robert G. Steele
Albert Whitman 1994
ISBN: 0 8075 1419 5
A young boy is woken by his flashing alarm clock, and with his father goes to watch the sunrise. Father and son communicate through sign language.
Lower Primary/7-9 years. HB. H.

DARK KNIGHTS AND DINGY CASTLES

Terry Deary, illus. Phillip Reeve
Scholastic (Horrible Histories) 1997
ISBN: 0 590 54298 2
Within the off-the-wall humour of the series is accurate and interesting historical fact.
Lower Secondary/9-11 years. PB.

DECEMBER ROSE, THE

Leon Garfield
BBC Young Classic Collection
A young sweep in Victorian London falls down the wrong chimney and involves himself in the teeming underworld.
Upper Primary. VHS.

DELILAH ALONE

Jenny Nimmo, illus Georgien Overwater
Chivers Press (Galaxy) 1997
ISBN: 7540 6014 4
With her owner on holiday, Delilah the cat decides to leave home, with catastrophic results.
Upper Primary/7-9 years. LP.

DIFFERENT KIND OF HERO, A	**Peter Leigh** Hodder/ALBSU (Livewire Youth Fiction) 1997 ISBN: 0 340 69697 4 *Ben joins the air force and trains to work on aircraft engines. He is also the victim of racial harassment. His heroic act saves lives.* Lower Secondary/7-9 years. PB. I.
DIMANCHE DILLER IN DANGER	**Henrietta Bradford**, illus. Lesley Harker Collins (book and tape pack) 1994 ISBN: 0 00 674881 3 *Dimanche is captured, but not concerned because her unusual friend is on the way.* Upper Primary/7-11years. PB. S.
DONALD AND THE SINGING FISH	**Peter Lubach** Macmillan Picturemac 1992. ISBN: 0 333 59308 1 *Donald catches a singing fish, and this wordless picture book relates his efforts to become a world-class entertainer.* Lower Secondary/9-11 years. PB.
DONALD GRAVES IN AUSTRALIA - CHILDREN WANT TO WRITE	**edited by R. D.Walshe** Primary English Teaching Association, PO Box 167, Rozelle, NSW 20039, Australia 1981 ISBN: 0 909955 35 2 *Graves was invited to Australia to present his theories on the process of writing in children and his development of methods that enable children to write with confidence.* Adult. PB.
DRAGON UPSTAIRS, THE	**Geraldine Kaye** Scholastic 1997 0 590 54285 0 *Anna knows very little English, and the discovery of a dragon's egg creates more problems than she can cope with.* Lower Primary/7-9 years. PB.

E

EARLY YEARS POEMS AND RHYMES

compiled by Jill Bennett
Scholastic 1993
0 590 53053 4
A collection of poetry suited to the interests and language abilities of early years education. A wide variety of subjects are covered, from animal and counting rhymes to homes and the seasons.
Adult. PB.

EDUCATING THE ABLE

Diane Montgomery
Cassell 1996
0 304 32587 2
Gifted children have special needs that must be met. This book assists teachers to develop criteria for identifying and helping able students.
Adult. PB.

EMOTIONAL AND BEHAVIOURAL DIFFICULTIES

Paul Cooper et al
Routledge 1994
0 415 07199 2
By considering the problems, devising solutions and putting those solutions into practice, this overview of some of the behavioural problems encountered in mainstream schools offers a concise guide to classroom and whole school management.
Adult. PB.

F

FARMYARD CAT, THE

Christine Anello, illus. Sharon Thompson
Hodder 1990
0 340 51398 5
A hungry cat creates chaos in the farmyard as she searches for food.
Infant/4-7 years. Large format PB.

FASTEST BOWLER IN THE WORLD, THE

Michael Hardcastle
Faber & Faber 1996
0 571 17355 1
Nick and his mother are cricket enthusiasts, but his father is not. Nick's ambition is to become the fastest bowler in the world.
Lower Secondary/11-13 years. HB.

FAVOURITE TALES
COLLECTION ONE
Ladybird Audio
Four stories - **The Gingerbread Man, Goldilocks and the Three Bears, The Three Billy Goats Gruff** and **The Little Red Hen** - read by a variety of entertainers.
These lively retellings are good for listening skills.
Lower Primary. S.

FIX IT WITH BUBBLE GUM
Ian Whybrow, illus. Tim Archbold
Orchard Books (Shrinky Kid Stories) 1995
1 86039 095 1
One of a series of stories about a shoebox farm. Art shrinks and enters the farmyard world. Large text with line drawings.
Upper Primary/7-9 years. PB.

FLAWED GLASS, THE
Ian Strachan
Methuen 1989
0 416 13492 0
Shona hopes for a miracle that will unlock her tongue and her body, enabling her to speak and walk. The answer comes from an American visiting her remote Scottish island home.
Teenage. HB. P.

FLOUR BABIES
Anne Fine
Puffin 1992
0 14 036147 2
Mr Cartwright's class are asked to look after flour babies (six-pound bags of flour) as part of the school science week, with devastating results.
Lower Secondary/9-11 years. PB.

FLYING FINGERS CLUB, THE
Jean F. Andrews
Kendall Green Publications, Gallaudet University Press, USA 1988
0 930323 44 0
Donald changes schools, and his first new friend is Matt who communicates through sign language. Together with a group of classmates they all begin to learn to sign.
Upper Primary/9-11 years. PB. H.

FOCUS ON THE CHILD
Judith Elkin and Ray Lonsdale
Library Association 1996
1 85604 109 3
A survey and analysis of the developments within library services for children and young people over the past two decades.
Adult. HB.

FOLLOW THAT CHIMP

Philippe Dupasquier
Walker Books 1992
0 7445 2511 X
A wordless picture book relating the adventures of a boy who helps a chimp when it escapes from the zoo.
Upper Primary. PB.

FOOTBALL STORIES

Michael Coleman, illus. Ant Parker
Orchard (Super Crunchies) 1997
1 85213 949 8
Very funny stories about the school team and the football cup.
Upper Primary/7-9 years. PB.

FOUNDATIONS OF LITERACY, THE

Don Holdaway
Scholastic, Australia 1979
0 86896 014 4
The beginnings of literacy approached from the viewpoint of developmental learning, looking not only at the theory but also the practical aspects of the classroom.
Adult. PB.

FOX IN LOVE

Edward Marshall, illus. James Marshall
Bodley Head 1982
0 370 30959 6
Fox has discovered girls, but the girls are not very interested in Fox.
Upper Primary/7-9 years. HB.

FRIENDS AT SCHOOL

Rochelle Bunnett, photos Matt Brown
Star Bright Books (distributed by Ragged Bears) 1995
1 887734 01 5
A photographic book showing an integrated early years classroom.
Infant/7-9 years. HB. P.

FROG AND TOAD ARE FRIENDS

Arnold Lobel
Puffin (I Can Read) 1983
0 14 031564 0
Frog and Toad are delightfully confused creatures who share enormous adventures.
Upper Primary/7-9 years. PB.

FROM BIRTH TO FIVE YEARS **Mary Sheridan**
Routledge 1997
0 415 16458 3
A guide to children's developmental processes which looks at the various stages between birth and five years. It includes information on initial tests for hearing and sight, and an index of support services.
Adult. PB.

G

GETTING STARTED IN   **Brian Cutting**
WHOLE LANGUAGE   Heinemann (NZ) 1989
962 291 376 8
A well illustrated practical guide to introducing the concept of whole language teaching into a primary school.
Adult. PB.

GIFT, THE   **John Prater**
Puffin 1985
0 14 05089 X
Without words, this is the story of a delivery and what happens, not to the contents, but to the box.
Lower Primary. PB.

GINGER NINJA THREE'S   **Shoo Rayner**
A CROWD, THE   Hodder (Read Alone) 1997
0 340 69380 0
Ginger Ninja the cat has acquired a girl friend.
Lower Primary/7-9 years. PB.

GODHANGER   **Dick King-Smith**, illus. Andrew Davidson
Chivers Press (Galaxy) 1997
0 7451 6974 0
The cruel gamekeeper has frightened the animals into submission, but reckons without the mysterious Skymaster bird.
Lower Secondary/9-11 years. LP.

GOLDEN BIRD, THE   **Berlie Doherty**, illus. John Lawrence
Heinemann (Banana Books) 1995
0 434 96799 8
Andrew stutters and tries hard to stay out of the limelight. A part in the school play shows his skills to the full.
Lower Primary/7-9 years. PB. L.

GREATER EXPECTATIONS   **edited by Eve Bearne**
Cassell 1995
0 304 33170 8
Children's reading and writing is explored and analysed to show how teachers can help children to become more critical of their own and others' writings. One section deals with the issues of oracy and literacy, culture and language diversity.
Adult. PB.

GUINEA PIG GANG   **Lucy Daniels**, illus. Paul Howard
Hodder (Animal Ark Pets) 1997
0 340 68732 0
The children wonder why Mandy won't join the guinea pig club. Another story about the vet's daughter.
Lower Primary/7-9 years. PB.

H

HAND-TO-HAND STORIES   New Zealand Federation for Deaf Children Incorporated, c/o Diane Wood, 16 Volga Street, Island Bay, Wellington, NZ.
Three well-known children's picture books are told in NZ sign language. Although some of the signs may be different, these stories are familiar enough to be understood by children using SSE or BSL.
Lower Primary. VHS. H.

HARRIET THE SPY   **Louise Fitzhugh**
Gollancz 1997
0 575 06462 5
Harriet wants to be a writer, so she spies on people and writes down what they do in her secret notebook.
Upper Primary/9-11 years. PB.

HARRY ON HOLIDAY   **Chris Powling**, illus. Scoular Anderson
A & C Black (Jets) 1997
0 7136 4829 5
Harry's holiday is certainly different, and he has plenty to tell his friends.
Upper Primary/7-9 years. HB.

HELPING CHILDREN WITH
READING AND SPELLING

Rea Reason and Rene Boote
Routledge1994
0 415 10733 4
A basic collection of suggestions for teachers and tutors working with children who have difficulty with reading and spelling. Photocopiable materials are included.
Adult. PB.

HELPING YOUR CHILD
WITH READING

Angela Redfern
Early Learning Centre and Reading and Language Information Centre, University of Reading.
A clearly laid out introduction for parents to enable them to help their child to develop the reading habit.
Adult. PB.

HELP! IT'S HARRIET

Jean Ure
Collins Audio
A collection of four stories about a very disruptive small girl.
Lower Primary. S.

HIPPO BOOK OF
SILLY POEMS

John Foster
Scholastic 1998
0 590 19251 5
New and old funny poems in an appealing collection.
Upper Primary/7-9 years. PB.

HOGSEL AND GRUNTEL

Dick King-Smith, illus. Liz Graham-Yooll
Gollancz (Read It Yourself) 1996
0 575 06376 9
A wonderfully inventive retelling of well-known stories with pigs as the heroes.
Lower Primary/7-9 years. PB.

HOW SCHOOLS
TEACH READING

Angela Redfern and Viv Edwards
Reading and Language Information Centre, University of Reading 1992
0 7049 0547 7
This lists and answers questions about learning to read which are often asked by parents and carers. Through explanation and example it demystifies the various methodologies in use in schools.
Adult. PB.

HOW THE LION LOST HIS LUNCH: Adventures with Jeremy James

David Henry Wilson illus. Axel Sheffler
Chivers (Galaxy) 1996
0 7451 6973 2
A collection of lively and adventurous short stories about the same small boy.
Lower Primary/7-9 years. LP.

HOW TO WRITE REALLY BADLY

Anne Fine, illus. Philippe Dupasquier
Mammoth 1996
0 7479 2023 9
When Chester realises that Joe is the messiest writer in school he decides to offer his expert assistance. The partnership they form benefits both boys.
Upper Primary/7-9 years. PB.

HUXLEY PIG GOES FLYING

Rodney Peppe
Tempo Video
Four stories about the pig whose adventures were on television.
Infant. VHS.

I

I'M GLAD I'M ME

Sesame Street Home Video
The Video Collection 1987
Songs about a child that emphasise self-esteem and confidence.
Preschool. VHS. E.

I CAN JUMP PUDDLES

Alan Marshall
Puffin 1983
0 14 031651 5
The biographical story of a boy crippled by poliomyelitis who grew up to become a full-time writer.
Adult. PB. P.

I WONDER WHO LIVES UPSTAIRS

Edel Wignell, illus. Leanne Argent
Cygnet Books, University of Western Australia. 1993
1 875560 19 X
Sophie wonders who lives in the flat upstairs. She sees a dog and knows that pets are not allowed. Hannibal is a hearing dog.
Lower Primary/7-9 years. HB. H.

**INVASION OF THE
DINNER LADIES**

Michaela Morgan, illus. Dee Shulman
A & C Black (Jumbo Jets) 1997
0 7136 4651 9
*Two modern dinner ladies replace the one everyone knows,
and the food changes for the worse.*
Lower Primary/7-9 years, HB.

INVITATIONS

Regie Routman
Heinemann, USA 1991
0 435 08578 6
*Offering suggestions to teachers, this covers strategies,
demonstration lessons, and an introduction to current
educational theories and practices.*
Adult. PB.

IT TAKES TWO TO TALK

Ayala Manolson
Hanen Centre, Canada (distributed by Winslow,
Telford Road, Bicester, Oxon OX6 OTS) 1992
0 921145 02 0
*Simple practical suggestions to use to encourage children to
talk and communicate. The focus is on using everyday
situations to enhance interaction. Reading and books play a
prominent part.*
Adult. PB.

IZZY, WILLY-NILLY

Cynthia Voigt
Collins 1987
0 00 184422 9
*A car crash leaves Izzy an amputee, unable to walk
without crutches.*
Teenage/11-13 years. PB. P.

J

JEREMIAH LEARNS TO READ **Jo Ellen Bogart**
North Winds Press (Scholastic, Canada) 1997
0 590 24927 4
*Not everyone learns to read as a child. Jeremiah has learnt
many skills in his long life, but reading isn't one of them.
He returns to school and trades some of his skills for help
with reading.*
Upper Primary/7-9 years. HB. L.

JESSY AND THE BRIDESMAID'S DRESS	**Rachel Anderson**, illus. Shelagh McNicholas

JESSY AND THE BRIDESMAID'S DRESS
Rachel Anderson, illus. Shelagh McNicholas
Collins (Jets) 1994
0 00 674493 1
Jessy has Down's Syndrome and is exciting at being invited to be a bridesmaid at her teacher's wedding.
Lower Primary/7-9 years. PB. I.

JUNGLE BOOK, THE
Walt Disney Video.
The video of the well-known film of the Kipling stories. This edition has hidden captions which can be activated by a caption reader.
Lower Primary. VHS (captioned). H.

K

KATIE MORAG AND THE TWO GRANDMOTHERS
Mairi Hedderwick
Longman (Oliver & Boyd) 1989
0 05 004407 9
One granny from the mainland and one granny from an island, and Katie Morag loves them both and enjoys their differences.
Lower Primary/7-9 years. Large format PB.

KEEPING IN TOUCH
edited Nigel Hall and Anne Robinson
Hodder 1994
0 340 58735 0
Geared to infant and lower primary, this presents ideas for using interactive writing to encourage and stimulate literacy.
Adult. PB.

KILLING THE DEMONS
Jay Ashton
Oxford 1994
0 19 271708 1
Sam is in a wheelchair following an accident that has changed her life. She blocks out her frustration by playing computer games.
Teenage/11-13 years. HB. P.

KIPPER'S BIRTHDAY　　**Mick Inkpen**
Hodder (Moon edition) 1993
0 340 6156 5
Kipper becomes very confused over the day and date of his birthday, and needs his friends to help sort out the problem. This contains interleaved Moon.
Lower Primary/7-9 years. M. V.

L

LANGUAGE DEVELOPMENT　**Irene Johansson**
IN CHILDREN WITH　Jessica Kingsley Publishing,
SPECIAL NEEDS　116 Pentonville Road, London N1 9JB 1994
1085302 241 1
This is a practical programme for parents and carers that encourages the development of speech and communications skills in children who have severe language delay.
Adult. PB.

LANGUAGE FOR BEN　**Lorraine Fletcher**
Souvenir Press 1987
0 285 65031 9
Ben's parents fight to have him educated through sign language, meeting with opposition and prejudice on all sides.
Adult. PB.

LANGUAGE IN COLOUR　**Moira Andrew**
Belair Publications 1989
0 947882 10 3
Themes for teaching environmental studies in the primary school, using poetry as the starting point.
Adult. PB.

LAVENDER'S BLUE　**Kathleen Lines**, illus. Harold Jones
Oxford 1954
0 19 279537 6
A classic nursery rhyme collection, which also includes some games, and is fully indexed.
Adult. HB.

LEARNING LANGUAGE AND LOVING IT

Elaine Weitzman
Hanen Centre (distributed by Winslow Press, Telford Road, Bicester, Oxon OX6 OTS) 1992
0 921145 03 9
The Hanen Centre is an internationally recognised organisation working with children who need extensive assistance with language learning.
Adult. PB.

LISTENER, THE

Elizabeth Laird, illus. Pauline Hazelwood
A & C Black (Graffix) 1997
0 7136 4709 4
An adventure story in comic book style, about Gavin and his missing Gran. He is helped by Shelley, who is deaf.
Lower Secondary/7-9 years. PB. H.

LITERACY AND LANGUAGE IN THE PRIMARY YEARS

David Wray and Jane Medwell
Routledge 1991
0 415 04211 9
An holistic approach to literacy and language acquisition covering learning across the primary curriculum.
Adult. PB.

LITERACY GOES TO SCHOOL

Jo Weinberger
Paul Chapman Publishing, 144 Liverpool Road, London N1 1LA 1996
1 85396 292 9
Explains the role of parents in the process of literacy learning, and demonstrates how much effective teaching takes place within the context of everyday family life.
Adult. PB.

LITERACY THROUGH SYMBOLS

Tina Detheridge and Mike Detheridge
David Fulton 1997
1 85346 483 X
Of interest to teachers, carers and assistants, this gives an overview of the ways in which symbols can be used to stimulate and increase literacy skills.
Adult. PB.

LONG SHOT FOR PAUL	**Matt Christopher**, illus. Karen Meyer Swearingen
	Little Brown 1990
	0 316 14244 1
	Paul wants to be a member of the basketball team and his
	brother is determined to help, but must make his team mates
	accept a developmentally disabled pupil.
	Lower Secondary/9-11 years. PB. I.
LOVE IS FOR EVER	**Jean Ure**
	Orchard 1996
	1 86039 460 4
	All the agonies of teenage love, plus drama
	involving a runaway.
	Teenage/9-11 years. PB.
LOVE IS NEVER SILENT	Cinema Club video.
	Adpated from the novel In This Sign by Joanne Greenberg,
	this major award-winning film tells the story of a young
	woman who is the daughter of deaf parents and her
	struggle for independence.
	Adult. VHS.
LUCKY NUMBERS	**Clare Bevan**, illus. David Pattison
	Macdonald Young Storybooks 1997
	0 7500 2360 0
	A family wins the jackpot and buys a bouse, but lose their
	happiness.
	Upper Primary/7-9 years. HB.
LUCY AND TOM'S CHRISTMAS	**Shirley Hughes**
	Longman (Oliver & Boyd) 1989
	0 05 004509 1
	A traditional English Christmas gradually gathers
	momentum as the two children make their preparations.
	Infant/7-9 years. Large format PB.

M

MAKATON NURSERY RHYMES

David Benson Philllips
W H Smith Video
A collection of 19 traditional songs and nursery rhymes told and signed using Makaton signing.
Infant. VHS. SL.

MAKING FRIENDS WITH FRANKENSTEIN

Colin McNaughton
Walker Books 1993
0 7445 3002 4
Long and short poems, plus pictures, of all sorts of monsters.
Upper Primary/7-9 years. HB.

ME - SONGS FOR 4-7-YEAR-OLDS

Anna Sanderson, illus. Kate Sheppard
A & C Black (Song birds) book and tape pack 1997
0 7136 4532 6
A collection of simple songs with words and music about the body and the five senses.
Infant/7-9 years. PB. S.

MEG AND MOG

Helen Nicoll and Jan Pienkowski
read by Maureen Lipman
Puffin Cover-to-Cover audio tapes.
The well-known witch and her cat take off on their very first adventure.
Infant. S.

MIGHTIER THAN THE SWORD

Clare Bevan
Blackie 1989
0 216 92793 5
Adam has spina bifida and a vivid imagination. He fantasises that he is a modern King Arthur and involves his friends in an extravagant game.
Upper Primary/9-11 years. HB. P

MR GUMPY'S OUTING

John Burningham
Puffin (Feel Happy edition, Living Paintings Trust) 1978
0 14 050254 8
Mr Gumpy allows the children and some animals to go boating with him after certain conditions are imposed. This edition contains Braille and a thermoform picture.
Lower Primary/4-7 years. B. V.

MY BROTHER IS DIFFERENT **Louise Gorrod**, illus. Beccy Carve
National Autistic Society 1997
1 899280 50 2
An older sister describes the way in which she and her
family help her brother and help him to keep safe.
Lower Primary/7-9 years. PB. I.

MY FRIEND MR MORRIS **Pat Thomson**, illus. Satoshi Kitamura
Gollancz (Share a Story) 1989
0 575 05998 2
Mr Morris has a catalogue full of exciting items to buy.
Good word play.
Upper Primary/7-9 years. PB.

N

NICE WALK IN **Nan Bodsworth**
THE JUNGLE, A Viking Kestrel 1989
0 670 82476 3
The class goes for a nature walk in the jungle, but the teacher
ignores the agitated comments of Tim. The pictures show the
children plus a wheelchair being swallowed by various animals.
Lower Primary/5-7 years. HB. P.

NIGHTWING TOWERS **Laurence Staig**, illus. Doffy Wei
Macdonald Young Storybooks (Tremors) 1997
0 7500 2239 6
One by one the residents of Nightwing Towers disappear,
so Charlie and Freya investigate.
Upper Primary/7-9 years. PB.

NO GOODBYE **Marita Conlan-McKrenna**
O'Brien Press, Dublin 1994
0 86278 362 3
Mum has gone and the children are left bewildered, each
reacting in a different way to the situation they find themselves in.
Lower Secondary/9-11 years. PB.

NOT GUILTY **Brian Grant**
Reeds Limited, Penrith 1994
9 780951 855218
The terrifying consequences of a hit-and-run accident
engrosses two teenage boys, one deaf and one hearing.
Teenage/13-16 years. PB. H.

NURSERY RHYMES	Pickwick Video
	Seventy rhymes sung and told by a variety of
	well-known entertainers.
	Preschool. VHS.

O

ON FIRST READING
Frances James and Ann Kerr
Belair 1993
0 947882 24 3
Whole class work plus displays to use as a first step to
visual awareness, listening skills and phonic use, plus
context and meaning in print.
Adult. PB.

ONCE UPON A TIME
John Prater, words by Vivian French
Walker Books 1993
0 7445 2252 8
A small boy muses on his day, totally ignoring the passing
parade of well-known characters.
Lower Primary/7-9 years. HB.

OPPOSITES
Angela Bednarczyk, signs Emma Iliffe
Star Bright, New York (distributed by Ragged Bears) 1997
1 85714 097 4
This board book has English signs added to clear, colourful
pictures.
Preschool/4-7 years. SL. H.

OUT AND ABOUT
Shirley Hughes
Walker Books 1998
0 7445 0605 0
Pictures and rhymes showing the changing seasons and the
outdoor life of small children.
Infant/7-9 years. HB.

OXFORD YOUNG READERS' DICTIONARY, THE
Oxford University Press 1997
0 19 910427 1
This large print edition of a well-known and highly
regarded school dictionary is ideal for any child having
difficulty in using a dictionary.
Upper Primary/7-9 years. LP.

P

PAPER BAG PRINCESS, THE **Robert N Munsch**, illus. Michael Martchenko
Hippo Books 1982
0590 71126 1
Princess Elizabeth chases and defeats the dragon who leaves her nothing but a paper bag to wear.
Lower Primary/7-9 years. PB.

PATRICK **Quentin Blake**
Weston Woods Video
Patrick finds a violin on a market stall and begins to play it with astonishing results. This animated film has a music track, but no text.
Lower Primary. VHS. L.

PAY ATTENTION, SLOSH! **Mark Smith**, illus. Gail Piassa
Albert Whitman 1997
0 8075 6378 1
Josh finds it difficult to concentrate and hates his nickname 'Slosh'. His parents and doctor explain ADHD to him so that they can all work as a team to help overcome his problem.
Upper Primary/7-9 years. HB. E.

PICTURES ON THE PAGE **Judith Graham**
National Association for the Teaching of English 1990
0 901291 20 X
A detailed study of the importance of picture books in the learning-to-read process.
Adult. PB.

PIGLET IN A PLAYPEN **Lucy Daniels**
Hodder Audiobooks (Animal Ark) 1997
1 859 98935 7
A pig in trouble is the signal for Mandy to help in her parents' veterinary surgery.
Lower Primary. S.

POEMS IN YOUR POCKET **Debbie Powell and Andrea Butler**
Kingscourt (Literacy Links) 1989
0 947328 56 4
A collection of poems to share and read aloud.
Infant/7-9 years. Large format PB.

PONY IN THE PORCH	**Ludy Daniels** Hodder Audiobooks (Animal Ark) 1994 1 859 98560 2 *Mandy helps out in her parents' veterinary surgery. Each story in the series is based around one animal.* Lower Primary S.
POSTMAN PAT AND THE BEAST OF GREENDALE	**John Cunliffe** Hodder (book and tape pack) 1998 0 340 71332 1 *Postman Pat and PC Selby set out to catch a mysterious beast.* Lower Primary/7-9 years. PB. S.
POTBELLY AND THE HAUNTED HOUSE	**Rose Impey**, illus. Keith Brumpton Orchard 1996 1 85213 891 2 *Told in rhyming couplets and comic-format illustrations, this is one of a series of stories about a gang of animals always in trouble.* Upper Primary/7-9 years. HB.

Q

QUEEN LIZZIE RULES OK!	**Margaret Ryan**, illus. Wendy Smith A & C Black (Jumbo Jets) 1997 0 7136 4689 6 *Lizzie decides to help with the school pageant, which she regards as boring.* Upper Primary/7-9 years. HB.

R

RAILWAY CAT AND THE GHOST, THE	**Phyllis Arkle**, illus. Stephanie Hawken Hodder (Story Book) 1997 0 340 69993 0 *Alfie is feeling unwanted and decides to have a holiday.* Upper Primary/7-9 years. HB
RATHER SMALL TURNIP, THE	**Laurence Anhold**, illus. Arthur Robins Orchard (Seriously Silly Stories) 1996 1 86039 174 5 *A cumulative tale about a farmer and his wife.* Lower Primary/4-7 years. HB.

THE READING FOR REAL HANDBOOK	**Colin Harrison and Martin Coles**

THE READING FOR REAL HANDBOOK
Colin Harrison and Martin Coles
Routledge
1992
0 415 08047 9
An account of current theories on the teaching of literacy, including reading, writing, second language learners, and assessment.
Adult. PB.

READ WITH ME : AN APPRENTICESHIP APPROACH TO READING
Liz Waterland
Thimble Press, Lockwood, Station Road, South Woodchester, Stroud,Glos   1985
0 903355 17 5
A primary teacher outlines the theory and practice behind her decision to move from reading schemes to books to help children learn to read.
Adult. PB.

READING BY TOUCH
Susanna Millar
Routledge   1997
0 415 06838 X
This is the result of a research project into how people initially process Braille, and how their skill with words, meaning and spelling influence the processing. The main focus is on Braille, but Moon, maps and icons are also mentioned.
Adult. PB.

RED BALLOON, THE
Albert Lamorisse
Legend Video
The film dates back to the 1950s and is a fantasy of a boy, a girl and two balloons. There is no text, but there is a music track.
Lower Primary/4-7 years. VHS. H.

RED EYES AT NIGHT
Michael Morpurgo, illus. Tony Ross
Hodder (Read Alone)   1998
0 340 68752 2
Millie decides to teach her know-it-all cousin Geraldine a lesson she will never forget, but it backfires. Large text with line drawings.
Lower Primary/7-9 years. HB.

RHYME READING AND WRITING

edited Roger Beard
Hodder 1995
0 340 62731X
An introduction to the use of rhyme and alliteration in language and literacy learning. Contributors include poets, teachers and linguists.
Adult. PB.

RING-A-DING-DING

Jane Sebba
A & C Black 1997
0 7136 4423 0
A collection of ideas for exploring sound, rhyme and rhythm with children using both tuned and untuned instruments.
Adult. S. PB.

ROGER WAS A RAZOR FISH.

comp. Jill Bennett, illus. Maureen Roffey
Hippo (ClearVision edition) 1983
0 590 70095 2
A lively collection of poetry for reading aloud and sharing. This edition has interleaved braille.
Lower Primary/7-9 years. S. PB.

ROLLERBLADING ROYALS

Karen Wallace, illus. Russell Ayto
Hodder (Read Alone) 1997
0 340 68072 5
The circus comes to town and the royal pair swap places with the circus royals. Large text with line drawings.
Lower Primary/4-7 years. PB.

ROSIE'S WALK

Pat Hutchins
Random Century (Little Greats) 1992
1 85681 074 7
This classic tale of a hen pursued by a fox contains 32 words which tell part of the story - the pictures tell the rest.
Infant/4-7 years. PB.

RUBY

Maggie Glen
Red Fox 1992
0 09 986550 5
Ruby is rejected by the factory and has 'S' stamped on her paw. She knows it stands for 'special' and leads a revolt of the discarded toys.
Lower Primary/5-7 years. PB.

S

SADDLEBOTTOM

Dick King Smith
BBC Video, told by Jonathan Morris
An aristocratic pig family is dismayed to find they have given birth to a highly unusual pig.
Upper Primary. VHS.

SCHOOL TROUBLE

Lisa Bruce, illlus. Lesley Harke
Orchard Books (Dynamite Deela) 1996
1 86039 179 6
Deela has difficulty staying out of trouble.
Lower Primary/7-9 years. HB.

SEAL SURFER

Michael Foreman
Andersen Press 1996
0 86264 685 5
A baby seal is born, watched by a boy and his grandfather. The boy and the seal enjoy the freedom of the water, surfing and swimming together. On land the boy uses crutches and a wheelchair.
Upper Primary/7-9 years. HB. P.

SECRETS

Keep Deaf Children Safe, illus Emma Iliffe,
National Deaf Children's Society
0 904691 39 X
Questions and answers about secrets, from innocent childhood secrets to more serious secrets involving adults. Good basis for discussion.
Upper Primary/7-9 years. PB.

SEE YA, SIMON

David Hill
Viking 1992
0 670 84866 2
Simon likes girls, his friends and having fun. He's a typical teenage boy who happens to suffer from muscular dystrophy. He is also dying and he knows it.
Lower Secondary/9-11 years. HB. P.

SELF-ESTEEM AND SUCCESSFUL EARLY LEARNING

Rosemary Roberts
Hodder 1995
0 340 62049 8
A positive approach to working with young children both in education and within the family. It emphasies the need for positive encouragement to develop self-esteem.
Adult. PB.

SHOO FLY SHOO!

Brian Moses, illus. Trevor Dunton
Ladybird (picture book) 1995
0 7214 9644 X
A cumulative tale of the antics of a fly.
Lower Primary/4-7 years. PB.

SHOT IN THE DARK, A

Rob Childs
Scholastic (Time Rangers) 1997
0 590 13882 0
Soccer plus time travel leads the team into a medieval football match.
Upper Primary/7-9 years. PB.

SIGN ME A STORY

Royal School for the Deaf,
Ashbourne Road, Derby DE22 3BH.
Eight stories told in British Sign Language by both children and adults. The settings are suitable to the stories and the storytellers dress appropriately. These are traditional stories which could assist with receptive skills.
Upper Primary. VHS. H. SL.

SINCE DAD LEFT

Caroline Binch
Frances Lincoln 1998
0 7112 1178 7
Sid's parents have separated and his is very angry. Mum lives in a conventional house in the country, Dad lives in a bender.
Lower Primary/7-9 years. HB.

SOLUTIONS FOR SPECIFIC LEARNING DIFFICULTIES

Jan Poustie
Next Generation17 Medway Close
Taunton, Somerset TA1 2NS 1997
1 901544 00 1
An identification guide to a wide range of learning difficulties with advice for further help and support, plus recommended reading.
Adult. PB.

SOMEONE LIKE ME

Elaine Forrestal
Puffin 1996
0 14 038644 0
Tas has an eventful school life, always in trouble. His love of classical music and his piano playing result in an audition at a secondary school specialising in music. The letter with the offer of a scholarship arrives and he can't read it because he is blind.
Upper Primary/9-11 years. PB. V.

SPEAKING AND LISTENING

Louis Fidge
Folens 1992
1 85276 193 8
One of the Essential Guides series. This looks at speaking and listening skills and the child's development of language through narration, description, instruction, questions, prediction, comparison, imagination, interpretation and persuasion.
Adult. PB.

STINKER MUGGLES AND THE DAZZLE BUG

Elizabeth Laird, illus. Susan Hellard
Collins (Colour Jets) 1995
0 00 675010 9
Using interactive text and illustrations, the reader learns how to handle the Dazzle Bug that has landed on Stinker.
Upper Primary/7-9 years, PB.

STORIES, SONGS AND POETRY TO TEACH READING AND WRITING

Robert and Marlene McCracken
Pegasus, Canada 1986
0 920541 35 6
This gives practical suggestions for assisting with the natural process of language acquisition in young children through the use of stories and rhymes. The technique can also be applied to older children.
Adult. PB.

SUMMER-HOUSE LOON, THE

Anne Fine
Chivers Press (Galaxy) 1978
0 7451 6971 6
Ione's life is changed forever when she meets the Loon in the summer-house. He also entangles her father in his extraordinary plans.
Teenage/9-11 years. LP.

SUNSHINE	**Jan Omerod**
	Kestrel 1981
	0 7226 5736 6
	A wordless story told in comic-book format working
	left/right across each double-page spread. Early in the
	morning a young girl begins to get herself ready for school,
	hampered by her parents' tardiness.
	Upper Primary. HB. L.

T

TEACHER'S PET	**Philip Wooderson**, illus. Guy Parker-Rees
	Orchard 1995
	1 86039 076 5
	The school is having a nature day, and Mr Tallboy asks his
	class to bring pets. The result is catastrophic.
	Upper Primary/7-9 years. PB.

THERE'S A HIPPOPOTAMUS ON OUR ROOF EATING CAKE	**Hazel Edwards**, illus. Deborah Niland
	Hodder, Australia 1980
	0 340 28697 0
	A little girl compares her life and living conditions with a
	hippo on the roof.
	Lower Primary/7-9 years. PB.

THIS IS THE BEAR	**Sarah Hayes**, illus. Helen Craig
	Walker Books 1986
	1 56402 494 6
	A bear is pushed into a bin by a dog and ends up at the
	dump, only to be rescued by the same dog.
	Infant/4-7 years. Large format PB.

TRAVELLING BACKWARDS	**Toby Forward**, illus. Ken Brown
	Chivers (Galaxy) 1997
	0 7540 6003 9
	The magic medicine Fanny gets for her grandfather has
	some astounding results as he regresses to childhood.
	Lower Secondary/9-11 years. PB. LP.

TREMORS	**Anthony Masters**, illus. Alan Marks
	Macdonald Young Storybooks 1997
	0 7500 2211 6
	A ship in danger, a disused lighthouse showing a flashing
	light, and a ghostly figure all add up to exciting adventures.
	Upper Primary/7-9 years. PB.

TROUBLE WITH THE TUCKER TWINS	**Rose Impey**, illus. Maureen Galvani Puffin 1992 0 14 054089 X *The Tucker twins are a menace. They bully other children and Mick finds going to school is no longer a pleasure. Mum offers a different way of looking at the problem.* Lower Primary/7-9 years. PB.
TWINKLE, TWINKLE CHOCOLATE BAR	**John Foster** Oxford University Press 1991 0 19 276092 0 *A lively and interesting collection of poetry for reading aloud.* Infant/7-9 years. HB.
TURBULENT TERM OF TYKE TYLER, THE	**Gene Kemp**, read by Michael Cochrane Puffin Cover-to-Cover Audio *Danny wants to move on to secondary school with his friends, but he is struggling to complete Year Six. Tyke decides to help, with some interesting results.* Upper Primary. 7-9 years. I.

U

UNDERSTANDING WHOLE LANGUAGE	**Constance Weaver** Heinemann, USA 1990 0 435 08535 2 *Whole language is a philosophy about the nature of learning and the teaching/learning environment which makes literacy central to all work and aims to develop literate students and lifelong learners.* Upper Primary/7-9 years. PB.

V

VERY HUNGRY CATERPILLAR, THE	**Eric Carle** Puffin 1974 0 14 050087 1 *A little caterpillar hatches one morning and spends a week eating his way through numerous foods. This well-known story is ideal for teaching the days of the week, the life cycle of a caterpillar and the names of different foods.* Lower Primary/4-7 years. PB. H.

VIDEO ROSE

Jacqueline Wilson, illus. Janet Robertson
Chivers Press (Galaxy)
1996
0 7451 4820 4
Sitting in front of the video with a packet of marshmallows is Rose's idea of heaven, until someone gives her the power to change her own life.
Lower Primary/7-9 years. LP.

W

WAY HOME

Libby Hathorn, illus. Gregory Rogers, narr. Greg McNeill
Random House (Australia), book and tape pack 1994
0 09 182729 9
A boy chases and rescues a small cat, talking to it as they progress towards home - a cardboard box in an alley.
Lower Secondary/7-9 years. HB S.

WE CAN SAY NO!

Sara Green and David Pithers
Tellastory
A fictionalised series of short stories about being careful and staying safe, aimed at helping children to be assertive and confident in dealing with potentially dangerous situations.
Lower Primary. S.

WEATHER WIZARD AND THE GIANT BREAD CATASTROPHE, THE

Jon Crame
Orchard (Super Crunchies) 1997
1 86039 450 7
Ruby adds extra ingredients to the clouds while her brother is away, and causes loaves of bread to fall from the sky.
Upper Primary/7-9 years. PB.

WHERE IS THE SKY?

edited by John Agard, illus. Andrzej Klimowski
Faber 1996
0 571 17942 8
An interesting and mentally stimulating collection of poetry which provokes discussion.
Lower Secondary/9-11 years. PB.

WHERE'S MY TEDDY?

Jez Alborough
Walker Books 1995
1 56402 468 7
A boy and a bear lose their teddies in the wood, with horrendous consequences.
Infant/7-9 years. Large format PB.

WHERE'S SPOT?

Eric Hill
National Deaf Children's Society/Heinemann 1986
0 904691 30 6
*A dual language editon of the very popular children's
picture book about a well-meaning puppy.*
Lower Primary/4-7 years. HB. S. H.

**WHISPERS IN THE
GRAVEYARD**

Theresa Breslin
Chivers Press (Galaxy) 1997
0 7451 5492 1
*A supernatural story of a boy trying hard to come to terms
with his own personal difficulties.*
Lower Secondary/11-13 years. LP. L.

WHISTLING JACK

Linda Newbery, illus. Anthony Lewis
Collins 1997
0 00 675295 0
Roger lives on a boat with hs master, but he hates tunnels.
Upper Primary/7-9 years. PB.

WHO SANK THE BOAT?

Pamela Allen
Nelson (Australia) 1982
0 17 006567 7
*A cumulative story about a group of friends out for the day in
a boat which eventually sinks beneath their combined weight.*
Lower Primary/7-9 years. Large format PB.

**WIZZIWIG AND THE
WEATHER MACHINE**

Geraldine McCaughrean, illus. Wendy Smith
Orchard 1996
1 86039 040 4
Wizziwig invents whacky machines.
Upper Primary/7-9 years.

**WONDERFUL STORY
OF HENRY SUGAR, THE**

Roald Dahl
Chivers Audio Books
*Henry Sugar pursues pleasure and avoids work. As with
many of Dahl's stories there is a twist at the end.*
Lower Secondary. S.

WORDS WITH WINGS

Moira Andrew
Belair 1991
0 947882 15 4
A collection of writing ideas for use with infant and lower primary classes. Various forms of writing are suggested from party invitations to poetry.
Adult. PB.

WRITING BOOK, THE

Pie Corbett
Stanley Thornes 1994
0 7487 1709 9
A comprehensive resource for language and literacy with photocopiable worksheets and ideas for their use.
Adult. PB.

WRITING: TEACHERS AND CHILDREN AT WORK

Donald Graves
Heinemann (USA) 1983
0 435 10271 0
Designed to help teachers in the way in which they approach children's writing, this covers the development of handwriting, spelling, concepts and the skill of revision.
Adult. PB.

Y

YEAR FULL OF STORIES, A

Georgie Adams and Selina Young
Orion 1997
1 85881 182 1
A story for every day of the year, including February 29.
Preschool/4-7 years. HB.

YOU AT THE BACK

Roger McGough
Puffin Plus 1992
0 14 034576 0
A selection of poems from 1967-1987 showing the breadth of this poet's work.
Lower Secondary/9-11 years. PB.

YOU CHOOSE

Keep Deaf Children Safe Project, illus. Emma Iliffe
National Deaf Children's Society
A series of questions and answers offering choice and stimulation for discussion on the subject of personal safety.
Upper Primary/7-9 years SL. H.

Z

ZOO IN OUR HOUSE, A **Heather Eyles**, illus. Andy Cooke
Walker Books 1988
0 7445 3648 0
*After a visit to the zoo on Sunday a new animal appears at
home every day of the week.*
Lower Primary/4-7 years. PB

Petunia was filled with joy. At once she began to work so that, one day, she could be truly wise. Then she would help make her friends happy.

LANGUAGE GAMES

The following is an annotated list of some of the language games currently available. Suppliers given were correct at the time of going to press, but they may change. The games listed can be seen and assessed at the REACH Resource Centre.

ABC/123 FLASH CARDS Ladybird Books,
Loughborough, Leics, LE11 2NQ.
Two sets of these bright cards can be used for snap using word, letter or picture identificaiton. Best used with young children.

CLINGING LETTERS Galt Education
(bulk pack) Culvert Street, Oldham, Lancs, OL4 2GE.
A polytub storage bin filled with 140 lower-case letters of the alphabet. Excellent for multi-tactile teaching of spelling and word order.

CLOWNING AROUND Philip and Tacey
North Way, Andover, Hants, SP10 5BA.
A board and matching pictures that can be used for visual discrimination skills. With younger children it can be used a number of times; older children will do it once only.

COLOR CARDS Winslow Press
Telford Road, Bicester, Oxon OX6 OTS.
These coloured photographs each have something wrong - clothing incorrectly worn, inappropriate use of equipment, a potentially dangerous situation. Very good for older children and those needing help with visual discrimination.

COMPARE BEARS Learning Development Aids (LDA)
Duke Street, Wisbech, Cambs, PE13 2AE.
These plastic bears were developed for teaching weight, counting and sorting, but are equally useful for teaching space concepts such as 'in front', 'behind', 'next to', 'beside', etc. They can also be used for colour sorting.

| **FUNKEY ALPHABET** | Keys to Learning, |
| **THINK LINK** | PO Box 379, Petervale, NSW 2151, Australia. |

Available from LDA, Duke Street, Wisbech, Cambs, PE13
2AE. *A card game based on alphabet sounds and
categorisation of sound. A decorative strip on each card
acts as a self-correcting mechanism.*

FUNKEY BLENDS Keys to Learning
PO Box 379, Petervale, NSW 2151, Australia. Available
from LDA, Duke Street, Wisbech, Cambs, PE13 2AE.
*The cards can be used to play snap, rummy and a memory
game. Each card contains a consonant blend and a picture.*

FUNKEY DOUBLE TROUBLE 1 Keys to Learning
PO Box 379 Petervale, NSW 2151, Australia. Available
from LDA, Duke Street, Wisbech, Cambs, PE13 2AE.
*A set of cards that can be used to play a number of games
based on two-letter sounds. Each game can be extended by
using double-trouble joker cards.*

FUNKEY DOUBLE TROUBLE 2 Keys to Learning
PO Box 379, Petervale, NSW 2151, Australia. Available
from LDA, Duke Street, Wisbech, Cambs, PE13 2AE.
*A second set of cards containing two-letter sounds that can
be used to play a number of games. Each game can be
extended by using double-trouble joker cards.*

FUNKEY MAGIC E Keys to Learning
PO Box 379 Petervale, NSW 2151, Australia. Available
from LDA, Duke Street, Wisbech, Cambs, PE13 2AE.
*Through the use of snap, rummy, fish and a memory game,
this card set concentrates on teaching the rules of final 'e'.*

FUNKEY READING Keys to Learning
AND SPELLING GAME PO Box 379, Petervale, NSW 2151, Australia.
Available from LDA, Duke Street, Wisbech, Cambs, PE13
2AE. *A card game based on word endings. The pack
contains a set of picture cards showing a complete word
used in a sentence, plus a set of word-ending cards that can
be used to play snap. Four alternative games are listed.*

LETTER LOTTO

Usborne Learning Games
20 Garrick Street, London WC2E 9BJ.
These are useful and adaptable games that concentrate on initial sound and picture recognition. They can be played with or without the accompanying board. Very good for use with deaf children as a way to teach and reinforce noun signs.

LOOK HEAR

Learning Development Aids (LDA)
Duke Street, Wisbech, Cambs, PE13 2AE.
A collection of everyday sounds on tape which can be matched to colour photographs. Because the photos include adults, they can be used with older children having problems with listening skills and sound identification.

MY ANIMAL ABC BAG

Fiesta Cafts
F19 Skillion Commercial Centre, Lea Valley Trading Estate, Cecil Wharf, Edmonton, London N18 3BP.
A zipped mat containing a tactile scene surrounded by the letters of the alphabet with an appropriate object velcroed to each letter. Ideal for children with poor fine-motor skills.

MY WORD

Waddingtons Games Ltd
Castle Gate, Oulton, Leeds LS26 8HG.
A pack of cards that can be used to build words. Each card contains four sets of letters, each made up of beginning and ending consonants, usually with a vowel. Players must match words wherever the cards touch. Very useful for mixed ability groups.

NEVER ENDING STORIES;
A STORYTELLING GAME

Living and Learning
Abbeygate House, East Road, Cambridge CB1 1DB.
This board game can be played at a number of levels. The cards are colour coded, and must be played onto the matching colour on the board. Each player must be able to use the cards to add to a sequential story. The cards are divided into characters, places, events, and actions. Wild cards are available, but should only be used when the children are accomplished at the game. The storytelling can involve any number of children working alone or in small groups.

PENTAGRAMS

Galt Educational
Culvert Street, Oldham, Lancs OL4 2GE.
*This comprises three sets of interlocking pentagrams -
consonants are blue, vowels are red. The popper system
allows the pieces to be locked together in any order to form
words. Once linked the pieces can be rotated thus allowing
a selection of CVC words to be formed.*

**PHON CUBES; WORD
BUILDING BLOCKS**

Phon Cubes
PO Box 140, Totton, SO40 7ZL.
*A simple and practical way to help children learn blends
and develop word-building skills. The set contains vowel
and consonant cubes that are colour coded.*

STORY FOURS

Philip and Tacey
Andover, Hants SP10 5BA.
*This pictorial sequencing game was developed for pre-
reading skills but works equally well with older children who
are having difficulty with sequencing. There are four boards
and four sets of pictures to match. Younger children match
picture to board; older children try to sequence the story
without using the board.*

**THINGS THAT GO
TOGETHER: THINK
AND MATCH**

Living and Learning
Abbeygate House, East Road, Cambridge CB1 1DB.
*Paired pictures that link together and are self-correcting.
Suitable for infants and older children needing intensive
work. This uses pictures to reinforce consonant blends.
Games include matching pairs, snap, rummy and
pelmanism. By using the letters in the top corner, the cards
can be sorted into sound-matched pairs.*

UPWORDS

Originally developed by Milton Bradley, now marketed in
the UK by other companies. Readily available in toy and
game shops.
*This is a three-dimensional word game using tiles that lock
onto a board. Words can be built laterally and vertically
allowing CVC blends and diagraphs to be built by adding
initial sounds. It can also be used to develop simple
crosswords.*

WORDSPIN

Geospace, distributed by Imperial Games Ltd, Southport PR9 ONY.

A hand-held game involving a sequence of eight interlocking wheels, each with ten faces containing a single letter. The wheels are spun to see how many words can be made up in a given time. The wheels can be separated so that the child works with anything from two-letter words to eight-letter words, depending on ability.

"He who owns Books and loves them is wise." repeated Petunia to herself. And she thought as hard and as long as she could. "Well then" she said at last "if I take this Book with me and love it I will be wise too. And no one will call me a silly goose ever again."

USEFUL ADDRESSES

This list has been abstracted from an excellent publication –
USEFUL ADDRESSES FOR PARENTS WITH A HANDICAPPED CHILD
by *Ann Worthington*, 10 Norman Road, Sale, Cheshire M33 3DB.
It is updated annually.

**AFASIC
(SPEECH IMPAIRED
CHILDREN)**
347 Central Markets
Smithfield
London EC1A 9NH
Tel: 0171 236 3632/6487

**BRITISH DYSLEXIA
ASSOCIATION**
98 London Road
Reading, Berkshire
RG1 5AU

CLEARVISION
Linden Lodge School
61 Princes Way
London SW19 6JB
Tel: 0181 789 9575

CONTACT A FAMILY
170 Tottenham Court Road
London W1P 0HA
Tel: 0171 383 3555

**DOWNS SYNDROME
ASSOCIATION**
153-155 Mitcham Road
London SW17 9PG
Tel: 0171 682 4001

DYSLEXIA INSTITUTE
133 Gresham Road
Staines, Middlesex
TQ18 2AJ
Tel: 10784 463851

DISPRAXIA TRUST
8 West Alley
Hitchen, Hertfordshire
SG5 1EG
Tel: 01462 454986

**ICAN
(INVALID CHILDREN'S AID
NATIONWIDE)**
Barbican City Gate
1-3 Dufferin Street
London EC1Y 8NA
Tel: 0171 374 4422

LIVING PAINTINGS TRUST

Unit 8 Kingsclere
Newbury, Berkshire
RG20 4SW
Tel: 01635 299771

NATIONAL ASSOCIATION FOR SPECIAL EDUCATIONAL NEEDS

Nasen House
4/5 Amber Business Village
Amber Close
Amington
Tamworth, Warwickshire
B77 4RP
Tel: 01827 311500

NATIONAL DEAF CHILDREN'S SOCIETY (NDCS)

15 Dufferin Street
London EC1Y 8PD
Tel: 0171 250 0123

NATIONAL LIBRARY FOR THE BLIND

Far Cromwell Road
Bredbury, Stockport
SK6 2SG
Tel: 0161 0217

NATIONAL SUBTITLING LIBRARY

3rd Floor Victoria Mill
Andrew Street
Compstall, Stockport
SK6 5HN
Tel: 0161 449 9650
(Voice and Minicom)

ROYAL NATIONAL INSTITUTE FOR THE BLIND

224 Great Portland Street
London W1N 6AA
Tel: 0171 388 1266

SCOPE

12 Park Crescent
London W1N 4EQ
Tel: 0171 636 5020

SENSE

11-13 Clifton Terrace
Finsbury Park
London N4 35R
Tel: 0171 272 7774